PONDERING LIFE

Chuck,
Hope u enjoy
Jim

JIM SHEEDY, OD, PHD

ISBN: 0615544126
ISBN 13: 9780615544120

Contents

Introduction – Why?

Have you ever really just wondered what all of..."this"...is about? And by "this", I mean life, God[1], and the universe.

I have been thinking about "this" for at least a dozen years. My investigation included study of various disciplines such as anthropology, history, religion, psychology, neurology, physics, and philosophy. My background as a vision scientist provided a firm platform from which to launch the investigation.

At first, my quest for the meaning of life seemed destined to be overwhelmed by the size of the task and the immense number of aspects to consider. But then, after looking at the problem from many sides, it started to come together for me. I began to write my thoughts on paper because it was the best way to examine my thoughts and seek clarity. Although I could not apply the same scientific rigor to my thoughts about the meaning of life as I do to my research into vision, I found that I could use reason to come to many conclusions. I had no initial intention of writing this book. However, the words on paper soon began to congeal into a cohesive statement about life that made sense to me. I want to share these thoughts with others who are likewise contemplating the meaning of life.

As a scientist, I have always adhered to the scientific method whereby a hypothesis is formulated based upon observation, and then an experiment is designed and implemented to test whether the hypothesis is supported. I have had to change my approach for this book, because the area of study is so audaciously immense. For this investigation, I have tried to remain

1 In this book, the word "God" is sometimes capitalized, sometimes not. "God" refers to a particular God and implies a central Creator and presence in the universe as taught by many . "god" is generic and refers to the general concept of a central truth or force.

as objective as possible and let the weight of the evidence speak. When the weight of the evidence indicates what is most likely true, then I must acknowledge some uncertainty but, at least for now, accept that which is most likely true. This is the only way to try to build a bigger picture with limited knowledge.

I have a request and a caution for the reader. Please be prepared to read these pages with an open mind. For one thing, this book accepts that life, including *Homo sapiens*, evolved on this earth. If you are unable to accept that as a possible truth, then this book is not for you. Readers should also be prepared to have an open mind about God and religion. . The writings in this book are not intended to be anti-religious nor anti-god. Religion has largely been a strong positive influence on our species and the argument for the existence of a Supreme Being or Supreme Intelligence is strong albeit inconclusive. I do conclude, however, that if there is a Supreme Being, then there is only one such God for our species. This concept is identical with the original premise of the God of Abraham, the first universal God who serves as the basis for 3 of the current largest religions on this planet (Judaism, Christianity, and Islam). The life truths that I propose in this book are also very consistent with Eastern teachings such as those of Buddha and Confucius.

I believe the reader will have a greater appreciation for the journey presented in this book if s/he knows where we are headed from the beginning. Here is a synopsis of the basis for our journey:

> *Vision developed very early in the evolution of life and from the beginning it was the most advanced neurological network. Cognitive skills and mind developed around the existing advanced vision neural networks. Most cognitive skills in animals and many of those in humans have developed around the neurology that receives and interprets vision. Most of the other human cognitive skills (i.e. those not associated with vision) have developed around speech and hearing – these speech-based cognitive skills, in their advanced forms, are entirely limited to humans. Furthermore, the survival instincts, needs, and desires associated with vision-derived cognition, in combination with the very different speech-derived cognition, can explain the long-term patterns of*

human groupings, as revealed in human history, and can also explain the fundamental characteristics of our present mind.

Homo sapiens are the most advanced form of Life on this planet. As with all other Life forms as we know them, our species and its groups (Civilizations) pursue something called "LIFE". Darwinian survival is simply the strategy that results from pursuing LIFE. With this understanding we can know the meaning of our lives.

It is my sincere hope that the words in this missive can provide you with insight and clarity about life.....and give you peace.

Satisfying a need,

Jim Sheedy, OD, PhD

CHAPTER 1

Our Human Mind

Introspection and Consciousness

We live, breathe and feel our individual-ness on a continual basis. Each of us has a consciousness that is very real and is the foundation of our existence. We each have a strong concept of "I" called the "ego". ("Ego" is the Latin word for "I".) This definition is consistent with the writings of great thinkers such as Descartes, Sigmund Freud, and Carl Jung.

The stream of consciousness that we each experience is experienced by our ego. If we introspect or try to study our consciousness, we fairly quickly conclude that it is filled with thoughts and observations.

We each have a strong sense of "self" or "ego"

Our stream of thoughts comes to us as an internal voice – as if in a conversation with our self. We can almost hear ourselves think. Our Right Brain, the essence of our awareness, experiences Life through its vision-based awareness of the things in its environment. The Left Brain then interprets those experiences and feelings into its language of words. For example, we can look outside at a snowy field with trees and a river, our right brain has a "feeling" of this environment that emanates from the deeper vision-based sense of "self". Our left brain then puts words around it. We can almost "hear" our left brain say "It's cold out there". We may also have a deductive thought about the snowy scene such as: "I should put on my heavy parka when I go out", or "I won't be able to jog outside today". These thoughts, which come to us as an internal voice, come from our left brain. The left brain is based upon the sense of hearing and processes information in a serial or sequential manner. Speech is located in the left brain. Our verbalized thoughts come from the left brain. These thoughts are effectively our "attention" to matters – whether they are objects in the environment or deductive thoughts. When we have thoughts, we are said to be "thinking". When we have a thought it comes from "I" or our individual ego.

Our ego observes and interacts with our worldly surroundings. Our body has specialized organs and systems with which we can sense the environment around us. These include the commonly recognized "five senses" of sight, hearing, smell, touch and taste. We also use our muscles to interact with our environment and manipulate objects within it. We perceive the "I" as experiencing and controlling all of these sensations and interactions with the environment. Many sensations and interactions do not reach consciousness unless we choose to pay attention to them. For example, when we walk down a street, we are not aware of the sensation of our foot impacting the pavement – but we CAN be aware of it if we choose to do so. Likewise, walking in a cold, snowy environment with a bright sun and the snow crunching beneath our feet creates an overall feeling for the environment. That feeling is comprised of numerous sensations including the coldness on our cheeks, the feel of the cold air in our nostrils, the noise of our feet crunching on the snow, the brightness of the sun, the feel of the snow as our feet break through the crust on top, etc. We may not be aware or think about any of these sensations, but as a whole they create a feeling. Most of these global feelings and experiences occur in lower brain centers or in the right brain.

Through introspection, we can be aware of the contributions of our right and left brains to our awareness and consciousness. The right brain is based upon the sense of vision and uses parallel processing. This parallel neurological organization enables the right brain to simultaneously process many pieces of information and assimilate them – very similar to processing a picture (i.e. vision). The right brain is sometimes called the "silent brain" because it does not have verbal thoughts. The right brain does not have verbal processing capability; therefore it does not have thoughts. However, the perceptions of the right brain are equally part of the "I" along with those of the left brain. The right brain can simultaneously process information from several different senses and create a holistic image or gestalt of a situation. When we say that we "understand" something or have an "intuition", this comes from the right brain. Such understanding or intuition comes about because the right brain has processed information from several different sources (i.e., several different senses or several different facts or deductive thoughts that have been processed by the left brain) and has come to a conclusion about something. Each of us has had the experience of toiling over a problem and after thinking about the problem and looking at it from every conceivable viewpoint; the answer just "comes" like a bolt of lightning. The answer can come to us when we are least expecting it – perhaps in the middle of the night, when showering, or having our morning coffee. The right brain has assimilated the information (from our left brain deductions) and given us the answer. Our feelings are also non-verbal aspects of our ego and are experienced by our right brain. The holism, understanding, orientation, awareness, intuition and feelings of the right brain are a strong part of our self-awareness.

Through introspection, we can be aware of the contributions of our right and left brains to our awareness and consciousness.

Ego, Death, and the Soul

Our ego, or sense of individualism, is extremely strong. Every existing moment of our life is experienced by "I". For each of us, our ego is based upon the activity of our brain and its interpretations of and interactions with the world around us. Our very strong sense of ego makes it easy for us to believe in a soul that continues beyond our death.

Our entire perception and understanding of the world around us is accomplished and experienced by "I". For each of us, our ego is the most fundamental and believable thing in life. Our ego feels so palpable that we can't believe it will die with the body, even though we know our brain is dependent upon the body.

The ego exists because of the inputs and actions of our body and the actions and interpretations of our brain. There is no solid evidence to support the concept that the ego exists independent of the body. Our primary observation in Life is that when a person dies, we no longer experience them. It appears as if their ego has died along with their body. Of course, we also can't refute the possibility that the ego (or soul) does somehow exist separate from the body, and some people report spiritual-type experiences with people who have died. We have such a strong sense of self that it is easy for us to believe that the "I" is somehow bigger than our body and that the "I" must continue after the body dies. Our ego is so tangible to us that it is almost impossible for us to believe that it ceases when our body dies. However, we have no evidence that the ego is in any way separate from our body or that it continues beyond the death of our body. In fact, from the preponderance of our observations, it appears that each person's ego dies when their body does. We see no remaining evidence of a person's ego when their body dies.

The most solid evidence we have indicates that our ego is intimately and totally tied to the body. Solely based upon observable evidence it appears that the ego is born when we are born, and dies when we die.

If there is something in the ego that continues beyond our death, it is referred to as the "soul". We have scant scientific evidence for existence of a soul.

Is the World Real?

There IS a real world that exists outside of our body. Although this point may seem elementary, it is an important one. Because our sense of ego is so strong it is tempting to postulate that only the ego exists and everything else is secondary. It can be philosophically argued that we can only be aware of our own existence or ego – and that the world around us is a product of our ego. Is it possible that our ego has fabricated the world that we observe and that the only thing that exists in reality is our ego? René Descartes (1596-1650), considered by some the father of modern philosophy, famously stated "Cogito ergo sum" ("I think therefore I am"). Our own existence is the most fundamental thing of which we can be aware.

However, it is wrong to conclude that the world does not exist. For example, we all can see the same tree. Now, I can't say that your perception of the tree is exactly the same as my perception of the tree. However, our perceptions are similar enough that if we were each to try climbing it we would likely start by grabbing the same branch. As another example, when you and I look at something that is "red" we will each say that it is "red". But does the sensation of "red" really feel the same to you as to me? We can never know this. It is for this same reason that we cannot explain the sensation of "red" to a person with color blindness.

Even though we cannot ever be certain about the similarities of our perceptions, we have very high confidence that our interpretations of the physical stimuli around us are quite concordant. We build highways and automobiles and are able to each operate the vehicles and navigate the highways similarly. Whether you and I perceive the highway the same is relatively unimportant. We are each able to perceive it in a way that our egos can interact with it similarly and in a manner that is (usually) not dangerous to one another.

> *There IS a common reality out there that we are each perceiving – we are not imagining this whole world in our mind. I am not imagining that you exist – any more than you imagine that I exist.*

Science has become our common language and method to analyze and assess the environment. Through science we have learned that the world around us behaves according to certain laws and rules. Science has been marvelous at validating and uniting our perceptions of the world around us, and science has become our method for establishing our accepted knowledge and understanding about the world around us.

> *We cannot completely refute the idea that the entire world is a figment of our ego's imagination. However, the life that we experience tells us otherwise. There IS a real world out there. And, through science, we have become increasingly clever at manipulating it to our benefit.*

Observing the World Around Us

Non-Human

The external world that our ego perceives is filled with an amazing array of objects – both inanimate and animate. We perceive the objects in our environment with our senses of vision, hearing, taste, touch and smell. Based upon the signals that our ego receives from our senses we are able to distinguish most of the objects in our environment from one another.

The objects in our environment generally fall into categories, and the relationship we have with each strongly depends upon the category. For example, our ego perceives rock, soil, clouds, and water as inanimate objects. We can admire them for their beauty and utility, but our relationship with them is one-sided. We perceive them as non-living things. We don't have a personal relationship with them. This is why the "pet rock", a 1970's fad, was so clever – the concept was an oxymoron.

The next level of objects consists of plants: trees, bushes, grasses, and flowers. We know they are living and we respect that. In many cases we provide care for plants – although this is usually in order to harvest them for food or building materials. We can also have a personal, or "feeling" relationship with a plant that we care for in our home. But, our relationships with plants are almost entirely one-sided. Plants are not mobile, and to our knowledge they do not see or hear, or have capacity to think. Our ego relates to plants, but we don't have any evidence that they relate to us in any way other than passively receiving water, sunshine, air and fertilizer, and occupying space on the landscape.

The lower animals are next – and what a wide variety among them! We relate to lower animals such as amoebae and insects similarly as we do to plants – we know they are living, we respect that, but we don't feel that they are relating to us. Next are animals such as fishes, amphibians and reptiles. We understand them to be self-directed animals with a brain. We can relate to them. We also know that, in a rudimentary way, they relate to us – if only to avoid us when they perceive us. We have a rudimentary shared relationship with these lower animals.

Following them are the birds and mammals – everything from ground hogs to squirrels to mice to deer to tigers to parrots to dogs and more. We can typically relate better with birds and mammals than to the fishes, amphibians and reptiles. We can make almost any mammal a pet or at least captive in a zoo or circus – and develop a behavioral relationship in which we both develop reactions to the other's actions. This is especially true for domesticated animals such as horses, dogs and cats. We clearly can assign to them an ego and mortal feelings; we even give them a name. We have a reciprocal relationship with mammals and we can identify with them. We even attribute human-like thoughts and feelings to them. These animals clearly have behavioral patterns and instincts. We know they are not our cognitive equals, but we can develop a caring and feeling relationship with them.

....And, then there are the apes, monkeys, and chimpanzees. When we come face-to-face with one of these primates, the relationship we feel can be considerably stronger than with other mammals. The human-like facial features and expressions cause us to also assign them human-like attributes. The relationship we feel with an ape, monkey, or chimpanzee encroaches upon the boundary between animal and human – which can be both intriguing and unsettling.

HUMANS – THE SENSE OF "GROUP"

And then we observe humans in our environment – animate beings that are the same as we.

And God said, "Let us make man in our image, after our likeness: and let them have dominion over the fish of the sea, and over the fowl of the air, and over the cattle, and over all the earth, and over every creeping thing that creepeth upon the earth". Genesis 1:26.

Our ego knows that every human also has an ego. The shared relationship has an overall sense of parity. We relate to other humans in a very special way. The relationship we feel with other humans usually transcends other relationships we have with objects or animals in our environment. The relationship with other humans has a sense of commonality and sharing that strikes to the core of our own ego.

We feel the sense of "group" with other humans. This sense is the same that other animals feel about their own species. It is similar to the herding instinct that exists in so many animals. In a Darwinian world, the sense of "group" is a necessary part of survival – required for defense and reproduction.

The sense of group resides in the vision-based cognition of the right brain. Human group abilities have transcended those of animals because of the contributions of our speech-based left brain.

The Human Brain – Right and Left

By far the big story about Homo Sapiens within the context of Life on this planet is our mental capacity. In a Darwinian world, our mental capacity has enabled us to ascend to the pinnacle of the survival pyramid. The human mind is what has separated us from the animal world and from Nature around us. Therefore, the essence of the story about our species centers on our mind. However, before engaging on the historical journey of the development of our mind, I would like to take the reader on a tour of some fundamental things that science has discovered about our brain and mind.

Our human history is the story of the development of our individual mind and our species' collective mind. The collective human mind has grown amazingly during our history; and it also serves as the base for that history. We all share the aspects of the brain that are shown below. We have mechanisms that enable collective thinking and agreement with one another (V.S. Ramachandran, 1999). Our cognition has grown rapidly and has exceeded any cognition in the animal world. Cognition is generally our sense of awareness and includes knowing, perception, reasoning, and judgment.

Our mind, of course, is located in our brain. The primary characteristic of the human brain that differentiates it from animal brains is our significantly larger cerebral cortex. A casual view of the human brain reveals two halves to the cerebral cortex, the left and right cerebral hemispheres. However, before discussing the cerebral hemispheres, let us have a quick review of the brainstem that lies beneath the hemispheres.

The Brainstem

Below the cortex lies the brainstem; it is older than the cerebral hemispheres in evolutionary terms. It has numerous named landmark features, but perhaps the most prominent feature of the brainstem is the collection of 12 cranial nerves that emanate from the brainstem. Memorizing these nerves is a primary part of any human neuro-anatomy class, and usually involves a pneumonic that begins "On Old Olympus' Towering Top, a...." Each of these cranial nerves is paired, i.e. there are right and left nerve pairs, and for each the brainstem contains a nerve center or nucleus that plays a major role in controlling the signals conveyed by those cranial nerves. The list of cranial nerves and the functions they serve is shown below.

1.	Olfactory	Smell
2.	Optic	Vision
3.	Oculomotor	Eye and eyelid movement
4.	Trochlear	Eye movement
5.	Trigeminal	Chewing, face and mouth touch and pain
6.	Abducens	Eye movement

7.	Facial	Facial muscles, tears, saliva, taste
8.	Vestibulocochlear	Hearing, equilibrium
9.	Glossopharyngeal	Taste, carotid blood pressure
10.	Vagus	Slows heart rate, digestion, taste
11.	Spinal accessory	Swallowing
12.	Hypoglossal	Tongue

The brainstem and its cranial nerves, which is an older part of the brain, serve many of the basic body functions, but not the higher levels of cognitive function that are the topic of this book. Considering the survival nature of evolution, the cranial nerves serve functions critical to the basic survival of the organism. The cranial nerves serve smell, vision, muscular movement of the eyes, hearing, taste and the initial stages of food processing. Most of these functions have been important to life survival and evolution going back approximately 530 million years to the Cambrian Period, to be discussed later.

The Right and Left Cerebral Cortices (Hemispheres)

The most apparent feature of the human brain is the two cerebral hemispheres. Parts of the two hemispheres control the basic sensory and motor functions of the body that are not already controlled by the brainstem. The skeletal muscles for our arms, legs, and most other portions of our body; and also the senses of touch, pain, cold, and heat are controlled by specific locations in the cortical hemispheres. The neural locations for sensing and skeletal muscle control are in contra-lateral hemispheres, i.e., the right side of the body projects to the left hemisphere and vice versa. This contra-laterality also applies to the right and left fields of vision and also the initial sense of hearing.

Although portions of the cerebral hemispheres serve muscular and sensory functions on opposite sides of the body, the higher cognitive functions of the two hemispheres are different from one another in a very different way. Evidence for this difference has been accumulating for centuries, but it was most profoundly demonstrated by the groundbreaking work of R.E. Myers, R.W. Sperry, and M.S. Gazzaniga in the 1950's and 1960's in studying epileptic patients in whom the corpus callosum and other connections between the two hemispheres were severed.

The corpus callosum is a thick bundle of nerve fibers that is the primary neural connection between the right and left hemispheres. In the early 1960's, the above-mentioned researchers performed surgical section of the corpus callosum to reduce the brain-wide spread of abnormal electrical discharges in selected epileptic patients. Study of those patients has directly led to our current understanding of the significant differences between right and left brain function.

The cognitive abilities of the right brain are based upon the sense of vision. It processes information in parallel – just as the sense of vision receives and processes an entire picture at once. All of the information in the picture is received simultaneously – i.e. in parallel. Because of this type of processing, the right brain can integrate information from several sources and arrive at an "understanding". The right brain has no ability to communicate or think in words – it understands concepts but cannot understand or communicate in words. The right brain is often referred to as the "silent brain". Feelings are generated and experienced in the right brain. Feelings are non-verbal expressions – poets and writers often try to attach words to feelings; but words always fall short of completely capturing the essence of a feeling.

The cognitive abilities of the left brain, on the other hand, are based upon speech and hearing. Speech and hearing are both time-sequential processes, i.e. information is processed serially, events follow one another. Hence the processing abilities of the left brain are serial. Our thoughts, which come to us as words, emanate from the left brain. Language skills are based in the left brain. Deduction and logic require sequential processing and hence are products of the left brain. Human ability to reason is based upon left brain activity.

In normal daily functioning, the cognitive abilities of the left and right brain are coordinated quite seamlessly. Each half of the brain has distinct abilities and strengths that may be uniquely used for particular mental activities. However, most mentally-guided tasks draw upon the blended abilities of right and left brain functions.

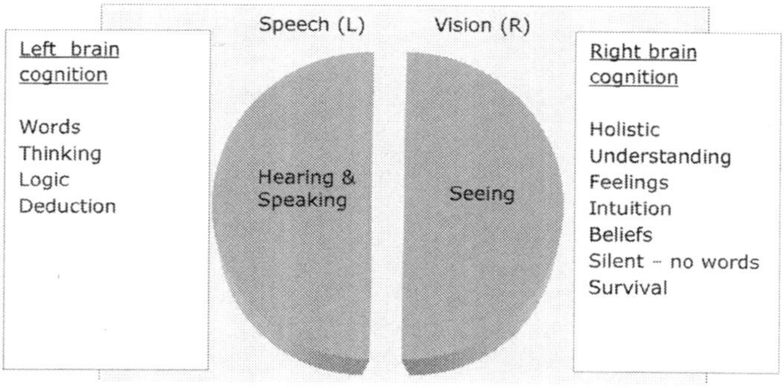

Figure 1. *A schematic of the left and right cerebral hemispheres and the cognitive functions they support.*

The corpus callosum is one of the last cortical pathways to fully develop physiologically, it continues development up to the age of 18 (Luders et al, 2010) and probably beyond. Development of the corpus callosum has been linked to learning. Late development of the corpus callosum also provides plausible support for the hypothesis that coordination of the right and left brains was accomplished late in evolutionary terms.

Caveat: This and further discussions in this book center on the differences between the cognitive skills that have developed from the neural architectures that serve the senses of vision and hearing. Visual and auditory perceptions are very different from one another and require very different neural architectures. Likewise the cognitive skills derived from visual and auditory perception are very different from one another. The fact that the left brain is better at processing auditory perception and the right brain better at visual perception has been established by scientific inquiry. The human brain is very complex and it is too simplistic to assign all visual perception and cognition to the right hemisphere and all auditory to the left. Some physiological exceptions can be found. However, to a very large extent the right/left separation is true and I continue to use those words in this book as shorthand synonyms for vision/speech based cognitive skills.

"Self" and Ego

The consciousness that we each feel is experienced by our strong *sense of self*, and by our thinking self – *the ego*. It becomes important to make this distinction between our sense of self and our thinking self. Our sense of self is non-verbal and comes from our vision-based (non-verbal) cognition. It is more fundamental than our thinking self or ego. Gerald Edelman, author of *Wider Than the Sky*, speaks of a primary consciousness that is the state of being mentally aware of things in the world, and a higher order consciousness that is the ability to be aware that we are aware.

> *There are two components to our consciousness and to the self (to which we attribute the consciousness experience): 1) a non-verbal awareness and sense of self that is based upon the sense of vision, and 2) a thinking awareness and sense of self (ego) that is verbal and based upon speech and hearing. They are distinct, but also closely linked with one another.*

If we introspect about our consciousness, we find that it is filled with a stream of thoughts that comes to us as an internal voice – as if in a conversation with our self. This left brain, or verbal aspect of our consciousness, is quite easily recognized. We can almost hear ourselves think. Our thinking self, or the "ego", is easily identified through introspection. It is so pervasive in our consciousness that it makes it difficult to be aware of the other aspects of our consciousness.

Our right brain sense of awareness is also part of our consciousness; however, it is often less obvious. Some people are able to discern the difference between the right brain awareness and the left brain thinking; whereas for many others their consciousness is so continuously filled with a stream of verbal thoughts that they are unable to appreciate the right brain awareness. A personal example of right brain awareness: when I am hiking in nature, or even driving on a highway, I am often simply appreciating and just being with the environment – no thoughts. I can even attain such a right-brain state with another person in the car, provided we are not in conversation. If I am asked: "What are you thinking?" My reply is: "I am not thinking about anything", because I have essentially shut down my left brain thinking and I am just "being" with my right brain awareness. I have found that some people cannot understand how a person cannot be thinking about anything; such people are unable to experience that state because their consciousness is continually filled with thoughts.

As discussed previously, the right brain is based upon the sense of vision and uses parallel processing. The vision-based parallel processing of the right brain enables simultaneous processing and assimilation of many pieces of information – essentially the same as processing a picture (i.e., vision). The right brain does not have verbal processing capability; therefore, it does not have thoughts. However, right brain feelings can stimulate left brain thoughts. The awareness contributions of the right brain are equally part of the self along with those of the left brain. The right brain sense of self is more fundamental to our being than is the left brain sense of self.

The right brain can simultaneously process information from several different senses and create a holistic image or gestalt of a situation. We continually have a general awareness of our environment. For example, you may be sitting in a chair in a living room with beige walls, a painting overhead, and a fire in a fireplace. You are very aware of all of your surroundings, but not thinking about any of them because you are reading or in conversation with someone. Your general sense of your environment comes from the right brain. Likewise, when we say that we "understand" something or have an "intuition", this comes from the right brain. Such understanding or intuition comes about because the right brain has processed information from several different sources (i.e. several different senses or several different facts or deductive thoughts that have come from the left brain) and has come to an understanding.

Right brain awareness, consciousness, and sense of self are attained during meditative states. The Buddhist teachings of "no mind" refer to the state of essentially shutting down the left brain thinking and ego, and just being with the right brain consciousness. In this state of mind, the original mind or true self is said to be attained. The Buddhist teachings very accurately identify the sense of awareness and sense of self that come from the right brain. The deepest part of our self is contained in our vision based right brain.

Because our minds can be overwhelmed by thinking and words, it is more difficult to access the right brain consciousness. As a result, the vision-based awareness housed in the right brain has often been labeled "unconscious" – by such scholars as Sigmund Freud and Carl Jung. At one level, this could simply be considered a semantic issue. However, I suggest that the act of "thinking" should not be the differentiator between conscious and unconscious. In fact, I suggest that the right brain sense of self and its contribution to our awareness is a stronger and more fundamental part of *who we are* as living beings than is our thinking left brain. These arguments will be developed in later chapters. Relegating the right brain awareness contributions to the realm of "unconscious" leads to the impression that they are less important than our thinking self. The general awareness and sense of self that come from the sense of vision should be considered a strong part of "consciousness". In fact, the right brain contributions towards creativity and understanding further suggest that it has leadership roles.

We can be aware that our consciousness and our concept of self are comprised of two portions: a right-brained sense of self that is non-verbal and based upon vision-derived cognition, and a left-brained thinking self that is verbal-based. On a daily basis, our sense of self and our thinking self (ego) are so in tune with one another that we don't generally recognize them as being different from one another.

CHAPTER 2

Our Vision-Based Mind (Right Brain)

Beginnings of Universe and Life

In order to fully contemplate life on this planet, it is important to understand the environment in which life has formed and developed.

The Universe – feeling small

The cosmos we are able to observe and measure with our eyes and instruments began nearly 14 billion years ago with a "Big Bang". The cosmos appears to be contained at its edges and there are estimated to be 3 to 7×10^{22} stars. In other terms, this is 30 to 70 billion trillion stars...a totally immense number that is difficult to imagine. There are also more than 80 billion galaxies in the cosmos. When we view the Milky Way at night, we are looking into the center of the flattened spiral that is our own galaxy. Our own galaxy contains 200-400 billion stars, yet the closest one to our own sun is Proxima Centauri, which is 4.3 light years distant. Our imagination cannot begin to envision the size of a Universe that contains 30 to 70 billion trillion stars. Yet, despite such an immense number of stars and the fact that we are in a galaxy of such stars, our nearest neighboring star is amazingly 4.3 light years distant!

Each of the above facts builds on the previous ones to reveal that our own little solar system is barely a grain of sand in a desert. Even so, our solar system is much larger than we can meaningfully grasp based upon our life experiences; the distance to the sun is 93,000,000 miles, or the equivalent of 38,000 trips from New York to Los Angeles.

Earth and Early Life

In 2001 the Wilkinson Microwave Anisotropy Probe (WMAP) was launched by the US space agency to make fundamental cosmological measurements of our universe as a whole. Analyses of those data have enabled a refinement of the age of the universe to 13.73 ± 0.12 billion years.

Numerous sources provide estimated timelines of the formation of the earth and evolution of life on our planet. The Earth was formed at nearly the same time as our solar system - more than 4.5 billion years ago. Therefore, our Earth is roughly 1/3 as old as the universe itself. The first known life on Earth, consisting of simple cells, occurred 4 billion years ago. Life has existed on planet Earth for at least 80% of its existence. The materials and conditions to support life existed relatively soon after formation of the Earth when the environment was still very hostile. The primordial mix of matter from which our planet formed and the conditions provided by planet Earth (as located in this solar system) enabled life to begin relatively soon after the Earth formed. Given the immense size of the Universe, and the relative ease with which life formed and has flourished on Earth, it seems very plausible, even likely, that Life exists elsewhere in the universe.

Here is a brief summary of the timeline (years ago) of Life on planet Earth:

13.7 billion	Big Bang, universe formed
4.55 billion	Earth formed
3.9 billion	First life on earth, simple cells
1.0 billion	cell colonies, sponges
570 million	Cambrian Period, complex life forms
300 million	reptiles

200 million	mammals
150 million	birds
130 million	flowers
65 million	dinosaurs died out
6 million	divergence from apes
100,000	*Homo sapiens* (humans)

For the first three billion years on Earth, life forms consisted of single cell organisms. The earliest forms of life existed in extremely hot environments such as around hot underwater vents heated by molten rock. These conditions would be unlivable for most current forms of life. These early single cell organisms derived their energy from the heat of their environment. About three billion years ago, cells developed photosynthesis to derive energy from the sun. About one billion years ago, multi-cellular forms of life began to emerge. However, these multi-cellular organisms did not have significant body forms. Organisms at this time were simple and composed of individual cells, sometimes organized into colonies such as sponges.

About 530 million years ago (mya) there was a huge advance in life forms. This was the beginning of the Cambrian Period which has been referred to as the "Cambrian explosion" and also as "Evolution's Big Bang". During the Cambrian Period there was rapid appearance of most major groups of complex animals. Most current living organisms can trace their roots to animals that developed during this period. Life in the Cambrian Period was exclusively in a water environment.

During the Cambrian period (530-490 mya) all parameters of the common basic body plan developed. These included a bilateralism of body design with a head, tail, appendages, gastrointestinal tract, notochord, and beginning of neural concentration in the head. Animals with jaws, mouths, teeth, claws and tentacles developed. Sexual reproduction, which laid the foundation for genetic variability and rapid evolutionary growth, appeared during this era.

A key attribute of the Cambrian life forms is the existence of hard, external body parts. Animal forms prior to this time had soft sides or tissues. Some of the animal forms that appeared in the Cambrian explosion likely had soft predecessors from the Pre-Cambrian period, but the remains of soft animals do not survive time as well as the hard skeletons of the Cambrian period.

Origins of Vision-Based Cognition

Development of Vision

The sense of vision developed and evolved in the Cambrian period. Vision is so fundamental to most of us that it is difficult to conceive that the world was once without vision. Until the Cambrian period, no living thing was able to see the environment. Until there was vision, there was only electromagnetic energy at a wide range of wavelengths, but there was no light. Light is defined as those wavelengths which can be seen by an animal. Without eyes to sense the electromagnetic wavelengths ... there is no such thing as "light". Light is a cognitive perception and was created during the Cambrian explosion.

The development of vision in the Cambrian period is documented by Andrew Parker's, "In the Blink of an Eye: How Vision Sparked the Big Bang of Evolution". He shows how the sense of vision developed very rapidly during the Cambrian period and how it drove the evolutionary process because of its immense survival value. Most developments in eyes are thought to have occurred over the span of only a few million years.

The evolutionary plausibility of something as complex as an eye is supported by the work of David Plachetzki, Bernard Degnan, and Todd Oakley (2007) at the University of California at Santa Barbara and by Dan-Erik Nilsson from Lund University (2011) in Sweden. Plachetzki et. al. described a current animal (hydra) that has no eyes but that can sense light because of light-sensitive proteins (opsin) on the outside of their body. Opsin serves as the basis for photo-pigments that are the initial light sensors used in animal and human vision. This finding that light-sensitive pigments have been found on the skin supports the Nilsson proposal for the evolutionary development of an eye. As a first stage, the opsin proteins form in conjunction with small pits in the skin of the animal. Because of the shadowing that occurs in a pit based upon the direction of the light, crude directional sensitivity is accomplished as shown in the illustration. With further development, the opening to the pit becomes very small, effectively creating a pinhole camera with greater directional sensitivity and even some imaging capability. Skin overgrowth creates a cornea (corneal tissue is derived from ectoderm similar to skin) and eventually we have a modern eye. Nilsson evaluated the rate of evolutionary change and determined there is more than enough evolutionary time for this to have occurred.

Role of Vision in the Cambrian Explosion

The sense of vision, today as during the Cambrian period, requires considerable neural networks to translate the signals received from opsin-driven nerves into a usable map of the world. Survival also required that the neural signals from the opsin-driven nerves be translated into muscle-driven evasive or attack movements. The nervous system that developed around the sense of vision was certainly the most advanced neural network in each of the successful Cambrian animals.

The strategy for evolution is "survival of the fittest". The importance of vision to survival cannot be over-emphasized. An animal with superior directional sensitivity and/or imaging capabilities will have clear survival advantage in a world in which animals can navigate their environment. Whether to find and locate prey, or to evade being such prey; vision was the primary sense used to guide the action of the animal. Parker suggests, with considerable reason, that the evolution of vision was the catalyst for the Cambrian Explosion. Attack behavior, guided by the sense of vision, also led to the development of defensive attributes such as hard exo-skeletons (armor) and camouflage.

During the critical Cambrian period the sense of vision, with its advanced and complex neurological network, was at the center of survival and fueled evolutionary development.

For each individual animal, vision provided an internal map of the external world. At first, vision was quite crude and provided only information about the direction of light. Even this, however, would be extremely useful information compared to not having it at all. As vision developed, the animal became able to identify images in the world around it. Prior to the existence of vision, possibly only the senses of touch, taste, or smell gave information about a world external to the animal.

Vision provided the animal with a view and map of the external world. As animals developed awareness of an external world, it necessarily invoked the concept that there was something inside the animal that was viewing the world. Self-identity of the organism was necessarily concurrent with the view of the external world. The animal navigated and interacted with the world using vision as its primary guidance and neurological system; the organism had to have some sort of self-awareness as it interacted with the visual world around it.

The concept of "self" is strongly encoded in the sense of vision and the neurological system that developed to interpret vision.

With vision, the animal observed other things, some which were fixed in the environment such as rocks and plants, and some which moved in the environment and served as either food or sources of danger. All of these required some sort of muscular response or action – if only to avoid collision. Navigation within the observed environment required an additional input: knowledge of the animal's body orientation within the environment with respect to gravity. This was accomplished through the use of a statocyst, which likely evolved as a small in-pouch of skin with some sediment that stimulated different areas of the pouch depending upon gravitational orientation. Vision, along with orientation information from a statocyst, enabled navigation within the world. Very importantly, survival of "self" was the primary objective of vision and its associated neurology as each animal strove to survive.

The concept of "group" also developed very early around the sense of vision. Vision was used to identify other moving things in the environment that were like its self. This was necessary for both survival and reproduction. There were survival advantages to being with the "group" of like organisms. There was safety in numbers and numerous ways in which groups of like animals could be more successful at survival in the hostile environment. Identification of like organisms was also necessary for sexual reproduction, which developed and flourished in the Cambrian period. Vision served the animal by identifying sexual partners – something critical to survival of the species. Therefore, both the concepts of "self" and the concept of "group", shown in the diagram below, developed around the sense of vision very early in evolution. Survival was the objective.

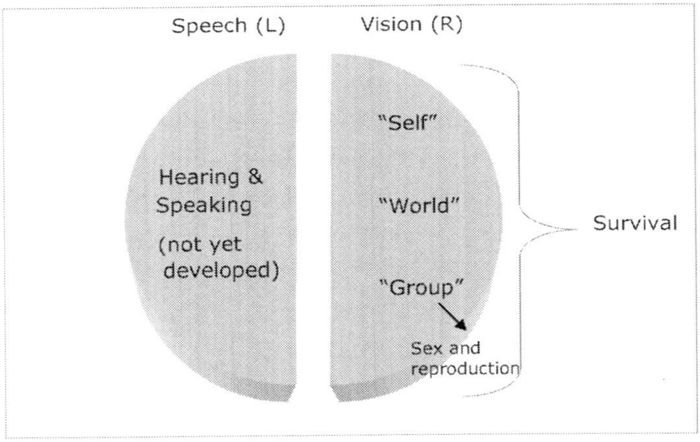

Figure 2. *Schematic diagram of the early Cambrian-era cognitive concepts that were based upon the sense of vision. These are foundational for the human right brain.*

In summary, during the explosive development of life forms in the Cambrian period, vision developed rapidly and played a major role in survival and continued evolutionary development. The sense of vision was fundamental to the concepts of "self" and "group", and it was also fundamental to reproduction and survival – the main objectives of the animal. These fundamental concepts or drives associated with the cognitive skills that have developed from the sense of vision remain a major part of Homo sapiens today (to be discussed later).

The sense of vision goes very deep into the evolutionary development of life. We share the sense of vision and many of the vision-derived cognitive skills with animals.

DEVELOPMENT OF COGNITION

From an evolutionary perspective, when and how did a mind develop? Somewhere between single-celled animals and Homo sapiens a mind developed. Our mind, consciousness, and cognitive skills reside in our brain. The brain is an accumulation of neural tissue located in the forefront or head of the animal. Such anterior accumulation of neural tissue first occurred in the Cambrian animals. It is unlikely that animals prior to the Cambrian period had any sort of mind or awareness as we define them today.

The first step towards developing a mind was probably a sense of awareness. As discussed earlier, vision gave the animal an awareness of "self" as distinct from "world". This would have developed gradually. In the earliest stages of vision development, when vision was really only crude detection of the direction of light, the neural signals indicating light direction may have directly guided muscle movement towards the light without any involvement of central neural processing or accompanying perception, i.e. it may have been reflexive. However, central neural processing certainly became necessary when the eye became capable of discerning many different directions and imaging became possible. Image processing required sophisticated neural circuitry.

Vision required more advanced neural processing for the animal than any other body function or ability. The strong survival value of vision provided the drive for better image detection and the neural capabilities to support it. The most advanced neurological circuits in the neural bulb at the head of Cambrian animals were most likely consumed with vision. The budding brain, based upon the sense of vision, was tasked with survival and was aware of "self" and "world". This was likely the beginning of awareness and mind.

Survival depended not just on seeing the world, but reacting to the images in the world. This required assessments of the patterns of light and darkness such as size, movement, direction, and other detail. Vision involves assessment of images or pictures. Image processing requires parallel processing of information – i.e. being able to simultaneously process information; and the neural networks that interpret vision developed around that capability. The animal's neural interpretation of the visual world would have affected survival and had an impact on the entire organism. The neural interpretation would signal "safe" or "danger" to the animal. It would also signal "group" or "other". As vision and image processing developed, so also did awareness of "self", "group" and "world". These basic recognition patterns were developed very early in the evolution of the animal mind and remain as fundamental concepts supported by our right brain. The growing skills at assessing vision images evolved into cognition that is based on vision. Such cognition includes feelings, emotions, instincts, creativity and understanding.

Cambrian awareness of the world was based upon vision and the neurological systems that evolved to support it. The minds of animals largely developed around neurology to support the sense of vision.

Animal and Human Vision-Based Cognition

Before humans there were no words and no thoughts. The animal world that existed before humans was nearly entirely governed by the sense of vision and devoid of words. The cognitive skills that had developed from the neurology of the visual system dominated the animal world – as continues today.

Animal and Human Consciousness

Animals seem to possess many of the higher level cognitive attributes developed from the sense of vision. Animals have instincts that are right brain cognition and are non-verbal. Animals use instincts for just about everything in their lives – including gathering food, identifying and fleeing from danger, and procreation. Do animals have feelings – another right brain cognitive ability? I believe the answer to this question is also "yes". Most people with pets or other close relationships with higher-level mammals will attest to this.

Animals have instincts that support the survival of their species – they eat, reproduce, and fight or flee to protect themselves from death. They have a sense of individuality that enables them to navigate the environment. They have clear concepts of "self", "world", and "group" that emanate from the vision-based world. Animal and human consciousness share these concepts.

Animal and human consciousness both have a vision-based awareness of the world. Animal and human consciousness also share some of the advanced cognitive skills developed from the sense of vision such as instincts, feelings (probably), and perhaps understanding.

CHAPTER 3

Our Speech-Based Mind (Left Brain)

Development of speech and hearing

Much less is known about the evolution of hearing than the evolution of vision. There are some indications that sensing of sound, such as is the function of the lateral line in fish, occurred as early as 260 million years ago (mya). Reptiles sensed sound with jaw bones. A transitional mammal "Yanoconodon allini" lived 125 mya and was known to have a middle ear (Wikipedia, 2011).

The major evolutionary advance that separated humans from other animals was the communication established through speech and hearing. Hearing, by itself, does not separate us from animals because higher animals have a good sense of hearing. What truly separates us from the animals is our ability to have advanced communication using coordinated speech and hearing. Although some animals do have a form of speech and hearing, it is very crude by comparison. For example, birds communicate with different types of chirps and chimpanzees and apes are known to communicate with crude forms of speech. However, humans have taken speech to levels that are magnitudes beyond that of any other animal. It is safe to say that speech, as we commonly experience it, is unique to humans.

Many questions remain regarding speech development in humans. Speech may have begun even 3-6 million years ago, but with a lengthy intermediate stage from ape language to human language. The throat and ear bones of Neanderthals from 500,000 years ago indicate some ability for speech, although it almost certainly was not spoken as clearly as today. de Boer (2005) has analyzed the evidence concerning speech development and concludes that modern adaptations for speech developed between 1.5 million and 500,000 years ago. Late *Homo erectus* probably had some ability to speak, and early Neanderthals and *Homo sapiens* likewise could speak. The transition to the facial and neck traits needed for modern speech probably did not occur until only 40,000 years ago – at about the same time as significant human culture began. John Hawkes, an anthropologist at the University of Wisconsin, has found eight hearing-related genes in humans that show signs of having systematically evolved over the past 40,000 years; some of the changes may have occurred as recently as during the past 2,000 – 3,000 years.

Speech combined with hearing is a very recent evolutionary development and humans are unique in having developed it to advanced stages.

Human Evolution and Anthropology

The chronological development leading to *Homo sapiens* and our accomplishments is approximately as follows:

- 6 million years ago
    - divergence of apes and human ancestors from a common ancestor
- 3.2 million years ago
    - Australopithecus (Lucy)
- 2.5 million years ago
    - first stone tools
- 2 million to 50,000 years ago
    - Homo erectus

- 400,000 – 25,000 years ago
    - Neanderthal man
- 200,000 years ago
    - first appearance of Homo sapiens (us)

Our ancestral line diverged from the apes six mya. There have been more than 20 species of *Homo* since that time. As recently as 50,000 years ago there may have been four types of humans living simultaneously (Wells, 2003). All waves of human development and migration have come out of NE Africa, primarily the volcanic Great Rift Valley in current day Ethiopia. One of the greatest survival characteristics of *Homo* has been adaptability, and numerous climate changes such as ice ages have favored *Homo* survival and development.

The earliest ancestors were capable of upright walking (bipedalism). Many upright walkers are found 6 to 3 mya, although all also maintained good tree climbing ability. All Homos from this era have small brain sizes; brain size did not significantly increase until 2 mya. The famous skeleton Lucy is from the genus *Australopithecus* approximately 3.2 mya. The skeleton indicates that she likely was habitually bipedal, but still maintained good tree climbing ability. The first tools did not appear until 2.5 mya.

These earliest ancestors also had inefficient bipedalism and were better adapted for trees than walking, and they were only 3 to 4 feet tall (Lucy was 3'8"). At best, they had crude oral communication and probably no speech-based cognitive function. If we were to meet Lucy today, it is unlikely we would consider her to be "human" according to our daily operating definition.

HOMO ERECTUS

Homo erectus was the most successful *Homo* species in terms of longevity, surviving for nearly two million years. By comparison, we (*Homo sapiens*) have existed only 10% as long, or 200,000 years at most. *Homo erectus* was also widely dispersed, having emerged from Africa to spread throughout the Old World. *Homo erectus* is an ancestor of whom we can be proud. S/he had several advancements that made this a very successful intermediary, living from 2 mya to 50,000 years ago and spreading widely through the old world. Several ancillary species developed as offshoots from *Homo erectus*.

Homo erectus was tall at 6'. They also had developed an efficient bipedalism that enabled them to run and walk for long distances with reduced energy consumption. For the first time, there was a significant increase in brain size and the appearance of a Broca speech area.

Homo erectus was relatively hairless, which gave an advantage for long term running. They could cool down by sweating; whereas most animals cool down primarily by panting which is less efficient. This enhanced cooling mechanism enabled them to be persistent hunters and wear down their prey. They could easily stay within sight of prey because of their height and excellent vision and run the animal to its point of exhaustion. Homo erectus also had stone tools for the final kill. Some Bushmen hunt, this way today.

Homo erectus was a great hunter. But, he did not hunt alone – rather in small groups. And the small groups had a unique skill – the ability to communicate with speech. The level of speech would have been crude by today's standards, but as a new tool it increased their ability to obtain food. They also required additional food, because the larger brain used more energy and needed considerably more sustenance.

Homo erectus lost tree-climbing skills while at the same time achieving the above advances. Congregating into small groups would have been required for survival at night – perhaps in caves. They also may have harnessed fire for warmth, protection, and cooking. If they were able to cook it would have improved health and nutrition. Did they learn to be social around the fireplace?

It is difficult to know the *Homo erectus* level of speech-based cognitive skill. Making stone tools such as hand axes required decision making. Did they develop social skills – perhaps while hunting or cooking? Wells (2003) reports a skull of an elder *Homo erectus* with no teeth and evidence to indicate he had lived that way for some time. Did another feed him – perhaps even chewing food for him?

The *Homo erectus* set of attributes and skills enabled them to be very successful in Darwinian survival. They were among the first *Homos* to leave Africa, probably 1.8 million years ago. By one million years ago they had populated from the Caucasus to Indonesia and into Europe and China – they had successfully inhabited the old world. They may have still been living as long as only 50,000 years ago.

Homo erectus was a very successful animal. But, we would likely not consider them "human" by current standards. *Homo erectus* was still an animal living in a vision-based world and with a vision-based cognitive mind. While it is likely they had some communicative speech and some elementary speech-based cognition, it was probably not fully integrated into their existence. They had a well-developed sense of self and group based upon the sense of vision, but probably had not very strongly established the speech-based correlates of ego and group-think.

As examples, there is no evidence that *Homo erectus* buried their dead; a sense of ego causes us to bury our dead because our ego can know that we will die someday. There is also no evidence of jewelry, clothing, or body paint – all of which are also driven by ego. Likewise there is no sign of art or any advanced culture or items such as pottery.

> *The Homo erectus mind was likely still a vision-based mind. Speech, although crude, was a fantastic new tool that assisted their survival as an animal, but speech-based cognition had not been integrated as part of their mind. They were a successful animal that had a strong sense of group emanating from their vision-based cognition – just as other animals have a strong sense of group. Homo erectus was limited to existence in small groups that were not very different from animal groups. They had not yet developed a level of group think that would enable them to evolve beyond campfire or cave groups.*

NEANDERTHAL

Neanderthal lived in Ice Age Europe and western and central Asia from approximately 400,000 years ago to about 30,000 years ago. Neanderthal was an offshoot from *Homo erectus*, likely through *Homo heidelbergensis* as an intermediary. Neanderthal were well adapted for hunting during the ice age climate of Europe at the time. The Broca speech area appears very like ours – as does the frontal cortex, though the Neanderthal brain had slightly smaller parietal and temporal lobes. They most likely were speaking, although with reduced speech-based cognition. Evidence of some advanced culture has been found such as a flute made from bone and a sewing needle. There is also evidence of burials.

Neanderthals were mostly meat eaters, hunting large herbivores. Over approximately 100,000 years and throughout Europe, few changes appeared in Neanderthal. Neanderthals had no projectile weapons – they needed to get close to their game. Most Neanderthal male skeletons have multiple fractures – probably from needing to get close to their prey! Lives were tough and short; few lived beyond age 30. Neanderthals lasted for almost 400,000 years. By 25,000 years ago they vanished from the fossil record.

Of course, *Homo sapiens* is the most recent evolutionary development, first fossil evidence appears about 200,000 years ago. We have been evolving since that time.

Human Separation from Nature

We gained our separation from the animal world, or our ascendance to the top of the Life pyramid, through the development of our mind. Very specifically, this was accomplished by the acquisition of speech and the cognitive skills derived from it. We are aware of our mind and the consciousness we experience, but how does our consciousness differ from that of animals?

The feature that most distinctly separates humans from animals is language. Humans have a complex speech pattern and ability to hear and receive meaning in the spoken word. Some animals are also able to verbally converse with one another. Elephants, monkeys, dolphins and birds, among others, are able to distinguish the sounds made by other animals – especially those of their own species. Pet owners also know that dogs can distinguish some human words. However, no animals come close to communicating verbally in the same manner as humans. Speech, as we commonly experience it, is uniquely human.

Because animals do not have speech as we do, they cannot have thoughts in the same sense that humans do. Humans have a rich speech pattern that enables us to think inside our heads. Animals cannot possibly have thoughts in their head the way that we do. They do not have the skills to communicate verbally the way that we do and therefore cannot think thoughts.

> *Since animals do not have complex speech, and cannot think in the manner that we do, they also cannot have the highly developed skills of deduction and logic that are cognitively based upon the sense of hearing and language. Language and the thinking skills based upon language are what most clearly differentiate humans from animals.*

Thinking is a very large part of our consciousness; therefore, consciousness must feel very different to animals. Animals can only be aware; thoughts are not part of their consciousness. We humans can be both aware and think. Or, as stated by Gerald Edelman MD, PhD: "we are aware that we are aware". Through introspection about our consciousness, we can be aware that we are aware. This is our left brain being aware of the right brain awareness. Our left brain can verbalize and have thoughts; the right brain cannot.

When humans emerged from Nature, we emerged from a vision-based world that we shared with animals. Certainly sounds were important, but not nearly as important as vision in establishing the reality of the world around us. The sense of vision was essential for all navigation within the environment, and for identifying all of the essentials for living and survival such as finding food, avoiding danger, and identifying a mate. The left brain thoughts of humans became mapped on top of the right brain world from which we came; and which had previously completely represented the reality of the world in which we had always survived. The thoughts came from within – they came from and represented the "self" from the right brain. The left brain awareness of the right brain awareness of "self", has become the human ego. Animals don't have an ego, they only have an awareness of "self".

The Story of Adam and Eve

It is tempting to think of the "moment" when humans first developed thinking ability and our advanced human ego. Of course, it must have happened over a long period of time instead of instantly. We also have no hard evidence to document events at the time of our separation from the animals. However, we have the famous Biblical story of Adam and Eve which provides a description of human separation from the animal world. It is a description of the development of language and thinking.

The story of Adam and Eve has almost certainly been passed down to us from as far back into our history as oral tradition extends and the earliest writers could record. Many human cultures have long histories of verbal tales that are passed from generation to generation. Chinese and Polynesian peoples have passed chants along many generations, often chronicling an individual from each generation. This is also evident in the New Testament where lineage is documented as a long listing of people, each of whom "begat" the next. It is also likely that the early Greek writings were written from long-standing chants passed down from earlier times. The story of Adam and Eve certainly originated long ago – when we were considerably closer to our roots than we are today. It is likely a tale that lingered in the folklore of human civilization at the time of some of the first writers.

The story of Adam and Eve begins in the Garden of Eden, where we are at one with nature. There are two named trees in the garden: the Tree of Life and the Tree of Knowledge of Good and Evil. We can eat freely from the Tree of Life. At this point, we were harmonious with nature in a visually based world without words. Up until this point in time we had not developed thinking ability or human ego and did not see ourselves as separate from the environment around us. This was almost certainly the state of living things prior to development of human speech. Adam could eat freely from the Tree of Life and continue to be in harmony with and a part of nature. He could walk without clothes and not be ashamed – he could not "think" about the fact he was naked. In nature, prior to thinking and human ego, there was no judgment of good or bad. In nature, everything just exists. Thinking and human ego must be present in order to make judgment.

> *Before thinking and human ego, we were harmonious with nature and lived freely, equally and non-judgmentally with all other living things.*

When we were part of nature, we did not make judgments between good and bad. However, as soon as we ate the fruit of the Tree of Knowledge of Good and Evil, we separated ourselves from nature. Prior to the development of human ego (i.e. eating the fruit) there was no right or wrong. There is no right or wrong in nature – things just ***are***.

Only humans are able to think and therefore to judge – and this is a major attribute that separates us from the animals. Development of judgment coincided with development of human thinking, thinking consciousness, and ego. The ability to judge, or the Knowledge of Good and Evil which we obtained by eating the fruit, is a trait that gave us the ability of God: "And the Lord God said, Behold, the man is become as one of us, to know good and evil", Gen 3: 22.

And, what is the penalty that comes along with this God-like Knowledge of Good and Evil (or ability to Judge)? *It is death!*

> *"But of the tree of the knowledge of good and evil, thou shalt not eat of it: for in the day that thou eatest thereof thou shalt surely die." Gen. 2:17.*

The creatures in nature do not have thinking consciousness or ego – hence they do not understand or fear death. Life just ***IS***. Animals will do everything possible to avoid death because of the survival instinct, but they do not know that they will die some day and they cannot think about it. Humans fear death because we have thinking ability and an ego that separates us from nature. Our thinking ability and human ego are so strong that they necessarily lead us to a knowledge that we will die. The knowledge that we will die is terrifying to our ego, because our ego feels so palpable and permanent to us.

"And the eyes of them both were opened, and they knew that they were naked; and they sewed fig leaves together, and made themselves aprons." Gen. 3:7.

"And the Lord God said, Behold, the man is become as one of us, to know good and evil: and now, lest he put forth his hand, and take also of the Tree of Life, and eat, and live forever: Therefore the Lord God sent him forth from the Garden of Eden, to till the ground from whence he was taken. So he drove out the man; and he placed at the east of the Garden of Eden Cherubims, and a flaming sword which turned every way, to keep the way of the Tree of Life." Gen 3: 22-24.

In nature there is little concept of life and death. Living things just exist – without human ego there is no sense of a beginning or end to life. Life just is. When in the Garden of Eden, we could eat freely of the Tree of Life. But when we developed thinking and human ego we became separated from nature. We could no longer eat of the Tree of Life – we became aware of our own mortality and were forevermore banned from experiencing life without death. Life was no longer harmonious.

Interestingly, in the Story of Adam and Eve, God keeps the secret to life (the Tree of Life). We were once a harmonious part of nature and life, but when we acquired the knowledge of good and evil, we no longer could be part of the "way of the Tree of Life". Even today, the origins and meaning of life are our greatest mysteries.

The tale of Adam and Eve seems very insightful; however we must accept the fact that it is an allegory. The allegory focuses on a particular moment when Man became separated from Nature – when in fact the transformation occurred over a relatively longer period of time.

The story of Adam and Eve is part of the Jewish, Christian, and Islamic teachings.

Animal and Human Grouping

We humans have a strong propensity for forming groups. This grouping need ultimately comes to us from the vision-based cognition (right brain) that we share with animals. However, we have added considerable speech-based (left brain) complexity to group behavior.

Animal groups

We emerged from the animal world in which grouping behavior is very strong. Animal grouping is instinctual (right brain) and demonstrated by the herding instincts of grazing animals, the family units of many animals, and the special organizational qualities of ants and bees. These are instincts that are based upon the vision-based world of the right brain. These instincts go back to the fundamental Cambrian concept of "group" that developed around the sense of vision.

Many lower animals do not have any clear relationships with one another beyond mating. This is certainly true for lower forms of animals such as amoebae, worms and many insects. Nonetheless many animals bond with one another and have the concept of groups and families. Mate and family relationships are observed in many mammals. Herding is a common instinct among many mammals; this behavior is also seen in fish and birds. Some animals like bees and ants have very complex group behaviors and relationships that enable them to build impressive colonies. These relationships largely serve to protect the species and/or to further its propagation.

None of the collective relationships in the animal world compare in size or complexity to the groups created by humans. There is a major distinction between animals and humans in terms of their respective abilities to create something that is greater than the sum of the parts. While animals may bond together in order to improve protection or food gathering capabilities, humans have been able to develop civilizations that serve the greater good in much more complex ways. Humans have demonstrated an amazing ability to work with one another – an ability unmatched in the animal world. This is because humans have been able to use their speech-based cognitive abilities to establish "group thinking".

Human Groups

The earliest humans were hunter-gatherers – i.e., they relied on hunting animals and gathering food that nature provided to them. They lived in small groups and each group had to totally provide for itself. Considerable cooperation was required to provide protection and sustenance for the group and its propagation. They needed one another for protection and survival. This sense of community originated from their vision-based cognition coming from the world of animals. Each individual had a right-brain feeling of "group", shared with other humans, and tied to the survival instinct embedded in the right brain. However, they also knew that both individually and collectively we were different from the other animals around us. They had separated themselves from nature with their left brain thinking – both as individuals and as groups. They had become reliant upon one another. They also knew or sensed that they had mental prowess that exceeded any that existed elsewhere in the animal world – a world from which they had become inherently different. Collectively they were much stronger than they were individually.

In those early days, we were surrounded by a harsh and dangerous world. Survival of each human and their individual ego was dependent on the group. We developed a sense of "group-responsibility". Individuals within the group began to acquire knowledge or skills that could benefit the group. This information was shared with others and became part of the verbally-based "group think" that was overlaid on the right brain sense of "group" that is a fundamental part of human and animal cognition. Some humans became more skilled at hunting, others at food preparation, child rearing, or jewelry making. A group identity developed and each human felt commitment to the group.

The social organization of humans has progressed from small groups of individuals largely based upon family, to small bands of dozens of people, to tribes with hundreds of people, chiefdoms with thousands, and states with hundreds of thousands. Beyond the development of city-states and nations is the development of larger civilizations. Small bands and tribes of people still exist in what we consider the lesser-developed areas of the world. (Today we can also see small bands and tribes within larger groupings – such as Girl Scouts, Yankees fans, Porsche owners, etc.)

CHAPTER 4

The Sensory-Based Human Mind

The Basic Sensory Mind

In the earliest days of human existence, we evolved from the vision-based world of animals in which the concepts of "self" and "group" were fundamental to who we were as beings. As we developed speech ability, the speech-based cognition was mapped on top of the already existent and strongly embedded vision based concepts of "self" and "group". As developed previously, the left brain correlate of "self" is what we refer to as "ego", and the left brain correlate of "group" is "group thoughts" as diagrammed in the Figure 3. This figure serves as the fundamental structural base upon which the Sensory Mind grows.

Right Brain "Survival" becomes Left Brain "Success"

Vision has been a primary implement of Darwinian survival since the Cambrian period. The neural architecture derived from the sense of vision has played the major role in the survival of most species.

The primary advance of *Homo sapiens* has been the addition of the speech/thinking capabilities that have characterized our left brain. In the earliest days of our emergence, our left-brain skills were a fairly simple addition to our primarily right-brain existence and enabled us to become more successful at surviving. However, our new thinking skill eventually enabled us to conquer all other life forms on the planet and to harness the planet's resources in a way as never before. Survival seems now assured.

As our thinking left brain gradually assumed a heightened role in our individual and collective mind, and as we successfully conquered the planet, "success" became the goal of the left brain thinking. We humans, who are largely led by our left brain thinking, are driven by "success". Of course, "success" can be and has been defined in many ways.

Hence, the deepest motivations of the right brain remain "survival". Species survival is deeply embedded in the right brain (vision-based) architecture and always will be. Our left brain (speech-based), however, is driven by "success".

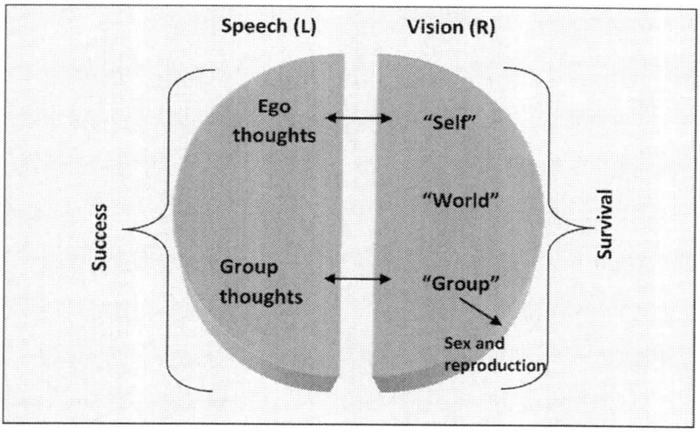

Figure 3. *The fundamental relationships of individuals within a species ("group") come from the vision-based cognitive world that existed before humans. Just as "ego" is a speech-based overlay on the sense of "self", "group thoughts" is a speech-based overlay on the sense of "group". "Group thoughts" are what has enabled humans to work so effectively with one another and to build civilizations. This serves as the base for the Sensory Mind. The speech-based cognitive skills of*

the left brain have enabled us to dominate life on earth. Survival of our species, the objective of the right brain cognition, is no longer challenged by the other forms of life on this planet. The objective of the individual and collective left brain is "Success" – as variously defined by human groups.

Greek Philosophy and the Sensory Mind

The Greeks

A good place to begin discussion of the modern mind is with the ancient Greeks during the era of approximately 750 BCE to 350 BCE. The Greek accomplishments during this time are sometimes referred to as the "Greek miracle". This was the first time in human history in which deductive thinking, reason, and logic prevailed in guiding human knowledge and civilization. Prior to this time, human affairs were largely governed by mystical beliefs about the nature of the world, i.e., human group affairs were largely still governed by the right brain prior to this time.

The Greeks formally developed the left brain thinking and reasoning ability, and established the rules of inquiry into life and science. They believed, and knew, that human reasoning could explain the workings of the world and did not need to rely on mysticism or gods. They believed that the universe was orderly, and they established the rules of science and mathematics. Nearly every scientific discipline today can trace its roots to the ancient Greeks.

One of the most enduring contributions of the Greeks is in the field of philosophy. Philosophy can be very broadly defined as the study of understanding the world. It is the study of general and fundamental issues such as existence, knowledge, values, mind, and our relationship with the universe. I suggest it is the study of……Life.

Philosophy….the early view of Life from left brain control

Even today, nearly 2,500 years later, Greek philosophy is still revered, studied, and considered to hold fundamental truths. Even though the Greeks are also known for launching numerous other disciplines such as engineering, mathematics, biology, chemistry, and physics to name a few. Why is Philosophy the one that endures as still being cutting edge? All of the other scientific disciplines keep advancing in their knowledge and sophistication. However, with Philosophy it is different. *Philosophy* is different because the Greek philosophers were looking at the fundamental truths about Life and nature. At that stage in the development of our human mind, the left-brain had a vantage point never again to be had. The Greek philosophers were close to and had a clear view of the developing human mind without the subsequent huge build-up of left brain group think that has steadily developed since then.

The Greeks were uncovering totally new territory. They were able to explore this virgin territory unencumbered by subsequent discoveries and evolutionary mind development. They were certainly closer to the core of operation of the left brain and its emergence from right-brain rule than anyone today could possibly be. Greek philosophy is still a standard bearer today.

Greek philosophy is best represented by the teacher/student Big Three of Socrates (470 BCE-399 BCE), Plato (427 BCE-347 BCE), and Aristotle (384 BCE–322 BCE).

Socrates was obviously a great mind and thinker. He was a great public orator, teacher, and he had strong influence on people. He never wrote anything down, however, and left that to Plato. Socrates also riled the powers of the time, which led to his sentencing to death by drinking hemlock juice.

The writings of Plato provide us with an amazingly clear view inside the human mind of 2500 years ago. Plato's greatest contribution is the Republic, and the best known passages are those of the Allegory of the Cave and the Analogy of the Divided Line.

Plato's Allegory of the Cave and the Analogy of the Divided Line each provide an introspective description of the vision-based right and the speech-based left portions of our mind.

ALLEGORY OF THE CAVE

In the Allegory of the Cave, Plato describes a Cave inhabited by a group of prisoners who face a wall inside the cave. Behind them is a huge fire and between them and the fire is a raised walkway on which people carry forms made of wood, stone and other material. The prisoners watch the shadows on the wall and are unaware of the forms that are casting the shadows.

According to Plato, the shadows on the wall are as close as the prisoners can come to reality. The shapes of the shadows are ever-changing and illusory whereas reality is contained in the forms that cast the shadows. According to Plato, we are those prisoners, trapped in a world of illusory images. The prisoners accept the shadows as reality in the world because it is all they have ever known.

The world of shadows is the world of vision. Plato even states that the prison house is the world of sight. With vision, shapes are continuously changing. For example, think of a table. The table can be viewed from a multiplicity of angles, and from each angle the table looks different; exactly as the shadows keep changing. However, in reality there is a single real table that is casting the shadows. The visual image of the table continually changes. The knowledge of the reality of that table is contained in our speech-based left brain. We give the table a name and know that it exists.

Plato continues the analogy by freeing one of the prisoners from the cave and describes the difficult adaptation this freed prisoner would have to the new world of reality to which he is exposed. This freed prisoner becomes enlightened by an entire new sense of reality. Plato likens this journey out of the cave as "the ascent of the soul into the intellectual world".

The Cave is the visual world of illusions from which we were imprisoned and from which we came. We emerged into the intellectual world of the speech-based mind. According to Plato, we can only know reality in the *intellectual*, or speech-based, world.

Analogy of the Divided Line

In the Analogy of the Divided Line Plato begins the discussion by stating there are two ruling powers and that one of them is set over the intellectual world and the other over the visible world. This analogy to our right and left brains could not be any clearer.

Plato further asks us to imagine a line that has been divided into two parts; he states that the two parts of the line represent the sphere of the visible and the sphere of the intelligible. The sphere of the visible is the world that surrounds us. It is a world of change and uncertainty and is filled with illusions and beliefs. Consistent with the Allegory of the Cave, we cannot know reality in this world; we can only have opinions. In the sphere of the intelligible, however, we have the unchanging products of human reason and intelligence. This is the world of reality in which we can have true knowledge.

Plato further divides each of the two-line segments into two divisions. Each sphere is essentially divided into a lower and an upper region. These lower and upper regions essentially refer to lower and higher levels of cognitive development in the two spheres.

Visible sphere:

- The lower level is comprised of images that are shadows and illusions.
- The upper region contains everything that we see including animals, other forms of life, and man-made items.

Intelligible sphere:

- The lower level is comprised of hypotheses and ideas.
- The upper level is comprised of principles and knowledge.

In these writings, Plato clearly differentiates our vision-based and speech-based minds. He also establishes lower and higher levels of development of both sides.

Modeling the Modern Mind

Plato's writings demonstrate how strongly our cognitive skills have been built upon the senses of vision and speech/hearing. Plato also observed that there are hierarchical levels of both the vision and speech-based cognitive development. As our human brain has evolved and developed, we have certainly had advances in our sensory-based cognitive skills. Hence there are lower and higher levels of cognitive skills based upon both the vision and speech-based neural architectures.

The model in Figure 4 shows the evolution of our Sensory Mind into higher cognitive levels. Figure A is the base as taken from the earlier differentiation of vision and speech based mind, and Figures B and C, respectively, model lower and higher levels of cognitive development.

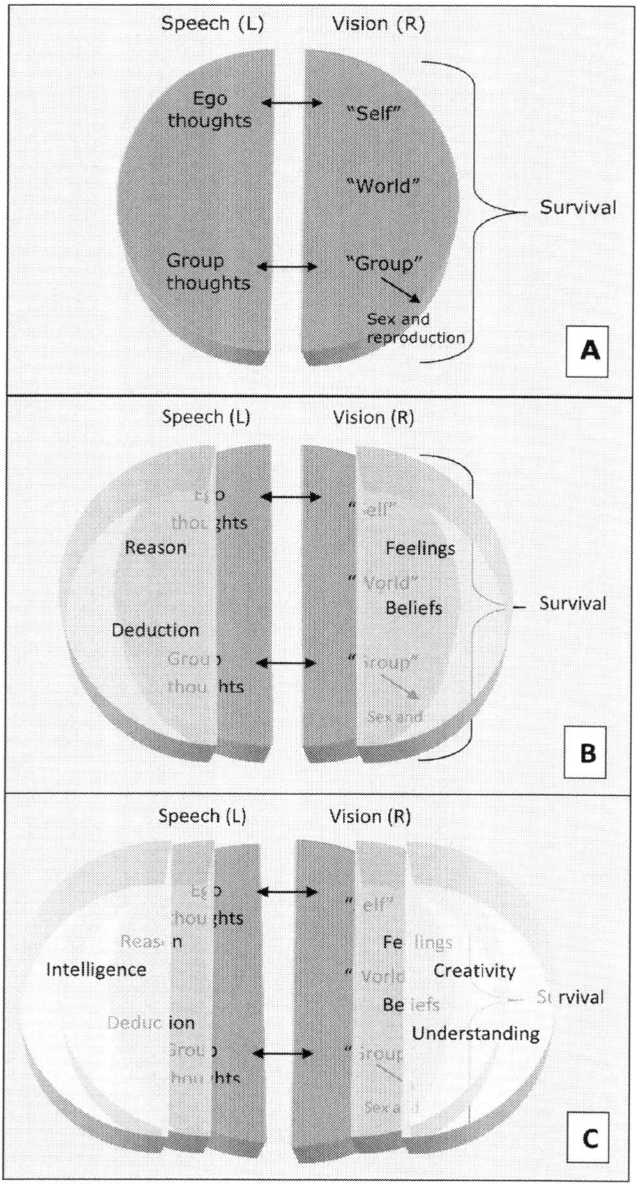

Figure 4. *A. The base for the Sensory Mind as developed earlier in this book. B. Adding lowest levels of cognitive skills to the sensory abilities. C. Adding higher levels of cognitive skills.*

Sigmund Freud and Carl Jung

Sigmund Freud (1856-1939) and Carl Jung (1875-1961) have most likely had the greatest and most recent significant impact on our thinking about the human mind. They did this largely in their quest to establish models of the mind in order to treat its maladies through psychoanalysis. Jung's theory of mind also led the way to categorizing people into groups based upon behavior patterns, specifically resulting in the Meyer's-Briggs Type Indicator test.

Freud introduced us to "id, ego, and superego". The id is rather animalistic and instinctually drives behavior in order to provide satisfaction or pleasure to the person. The id is unconscious and responsible for our basic drives and desires in life; it represents the vision-based cognition which is both unconscious and basic. The ego in Freud's world is where conscious awareness exists. The ego balances the needs of the id and superego and is where reason and common sense occur. Freud's definition of ego is very consistent with theories presented here. The superego has both conscious and unconscious elements, and is the higher level of behavior motivations such as morals, ethics, ideals, etc. (i.e. "conscience"). A superego conscience basically causes us to be a good citizen in the world and seems to have the sense of "group" as its basis. Therefore, since it is both conscious and unconscious, the superego straddles both our right brain sense of "group" and also our left brain "group thoughts". The approximate relationship between the Freudian concepts and the Sensory Mind is diagrammed in the following figure. The Freudian categories, however, are not as perfectly encapsulated as Figure 5 suggests. For example, part of Freud's ego is unconscious, implying that part of the Freudian ego also exists in the right brain.

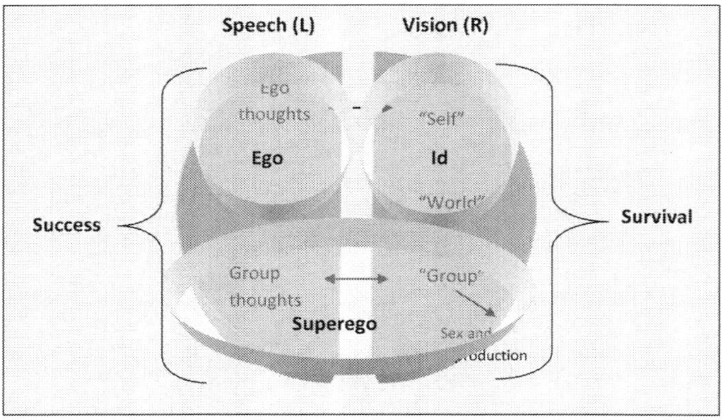

Figure 5. *An approximation showing how the Freudian id, ego, and superego overlay the base for the Sensory Mind.*

Freud is also remembered well for his psychoanalytic method of attempting to uncover the unconscious and reveal it to the patient. However, as pointed out by Boeree (1997), the unconscious is filled with "seething desires, perverse and incestuous cravings, and….frightening experiences", and may not be a humane place for a psychologically-challenged patient.

Sigmund Freud and Carl Jung, who was 21 years younger, had an intense academic exchange with one another for approximately 3 years, after which time they went their own ways, largely in disagreement. The two had significant influence on one another. Jung opposed experimental psychology and advocated that the truth about human behavior could be identified on the streets and by-ways, whether high or low, of the living world. He conceived his well-known theories primarily by observing people, largely from his psychiatric practice, and using his experience to perceive patterns. The teachings of Carl Jung have attracted a large following of both supporters and detractors (Boeree, 1997). The strong impact he has had on psychoanalysis and analytical psychology cannot be questioned.

Freud and Jung both believed in a hierarchical relationship between "unconscious" and "conscious". Clinical treatment was often directed towards making the unconscious conscious, i.e. delving into the unconscious of the patient. The Freudian and Jungian unconscious is analogous to the vision-based right brain. The right brain, since it has no words or thoughts, can easily be thought of as "unconscious". However, I suggest that our general awareness comes from our right brain and is part of the consciousness that we can appreciate.

The teachings of Carl Jung are numerous and broad within the field (Young-Eisendrath and Dawson, 1997). Here I will address two of his most significant and important contributions: 1) the divisions or parts of the psyche and, 2) his psychological types which led to personality typing and the Myers-Briggs Type Indicator test.

THE JUNG PSYCHE

Carl Jung divided the human psyche into three parts: the ego, the personal unconscious, and the collective unconscious. He is particularly known for his identification of the latter. Jung characterizes these as essentially descending levels of our psyche. The ego is the conscious and thinking self; the personal unconscious is the collective personal experiences unique to each individual, and the collective unconscious is a collection of experiences and behavior patterns that is common to all people.

Arguments about "consciousness" aside, the Jungian personal unconscious and collective unconscious are analogous to the right brain concepts of "self" and "group" developed herein. Likewise, the Jungian concept of ego is the same as the left brain ego in the sensory mind. The Jungian psyche categories overlay the sensory mind base in Figure 6.

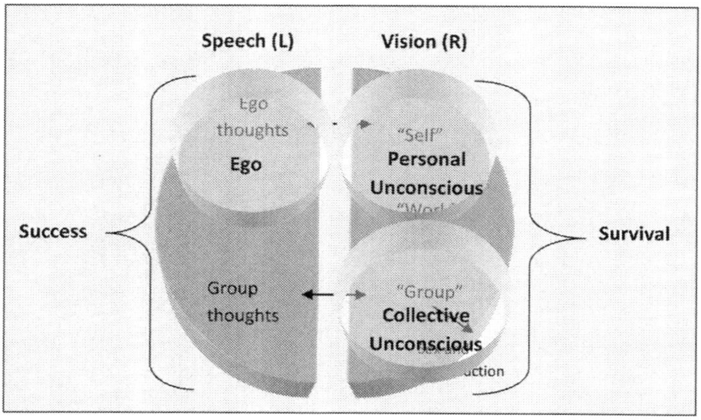

Figure 6. *The three Jungian components of the psyche (ego, personal unconscious, and collective unconscious) overlaid on the base of the Sensory Mind.*

The three Jungian components of the psyche fit nicely atop the sensory mind. In fact, Jung fairly precisely identified 3 of the 4 main aspects of the Sensory Mind; he did not identify the "group thoughts". I suspect that Jung would embrace the "group thoughts" aspect of the human psyche if he could now consider it. Jung also suggested a fairly strong hierarchical order from ego down to personal unconscious and finally down to collective unconscious. The hierarchical superiority of the ego over the right-brain sense of "self", at least in terms of our daily awareness, is acknowledged; the development of our speech-based left brain must be considered a significant advancement. The thinking brain superiority was also recognized by Plato. There is almost certainly also a hierarchical relationship between the personal unconscious ("self") and the collective unconscious ("group"). It is likely that many common group behaviors are encoded in our genes and are a part of all members of a species. This serves as a base from which each individual evolves their particular traits and behaviors.

Jung, Myers-Briggs, and the Sensory Mind

Jung also determined that people adopt certain definable modes of perception. These modes can be used to establish certain behavior patterns that describe psychological types. Jung defined 3 basic axes along which human psychological types can be modeled. Each of these axes has opposite traits at each end; the 3 axes are: introversion/extraversion, thinking/feeling, and sensing/intuition.

The first, and most fundamental, Jungian axis is introversion/extraversion. He considered these as two basic modes of perception. In introversion the psyche is oriented towards the internal world and in extraversion towards the external world. Jung considered this type distinction as the fundamental one for which others served as modifiers.

The Jungian introversion/extraversion distinction, or the separation between internal and external, is consistent with the original cognitive characteristic associated with the sense of vision in the Cambrian period. This is perhaps the deepest division caused by addition of vision to animals, which occurred at the very earliest development of an eye and sense of vision. For both survival and reproduction we relied on the concepts of "self", "world", and "group". The distinction between "self" and "world/group" was one of the strongest and earliest strategies employed for survival of our species.

Behaviorally, extraverts are outgoing and very communicative with others whereas introverts are inwardly oriented. Extraverts are oriented towards "world/group" whereas introverts are oriented towards "self".

The first Jungian axis, shown in Figure 7 is firmly atop the base level of the Sensory Mind; it is a solid fit. This axis also serves as one of the differentiating axes that are probed in the Myers-Briggs Type Indicator test.

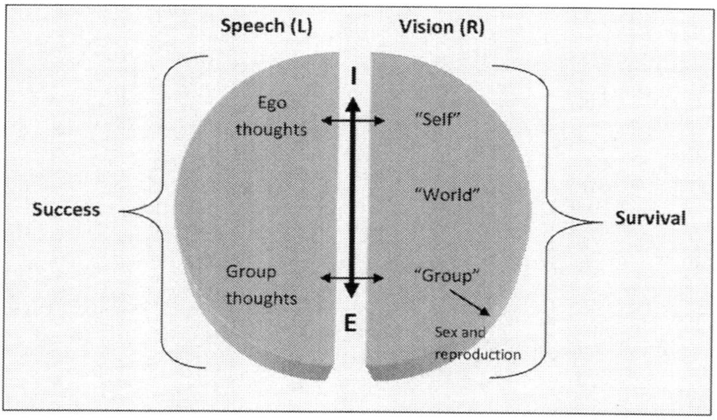

Figure 7. *The* **I***ntrovert/***E***xtravert fundamental Jungian axis overlaying the base for the Sensory Mind. The neural and behavioral bases for this axis date back to the development of vision in the Cambrian Period. The I/E axis is tested in the Myers-Briggs Type Indicator test.*

In addition to these two fundamental modes of perception, Jung also described four properties of consciousness that are paired opposites: thinking/feeling and intuition/sensation. These modes can be combined in various ways and result in personality types that can be used in clinical practice as well as in typing of normal behavior patterns.

The second Jungian axis is defined by Thinking – Feeling. This axis is defined as the judging scale.

- Thinking
  - Preference for deciding via objective impersonal logic
- Feeling
  - Preference for deciding via subjective and emotional responses

The Thinking/Feeling axis (Figure 8) is the orientation of the psyche to the speech-based left brain or the vision-based right brain. The distinction for preference to the right or left brain likewise is basic to our brain and its development. However, this axis did not form until *Homo sapiens* developed speech and set itself apart from the animal world. This is why the T/F second Jungian axis is shown in the figure at a cognitive level above the base sensations.

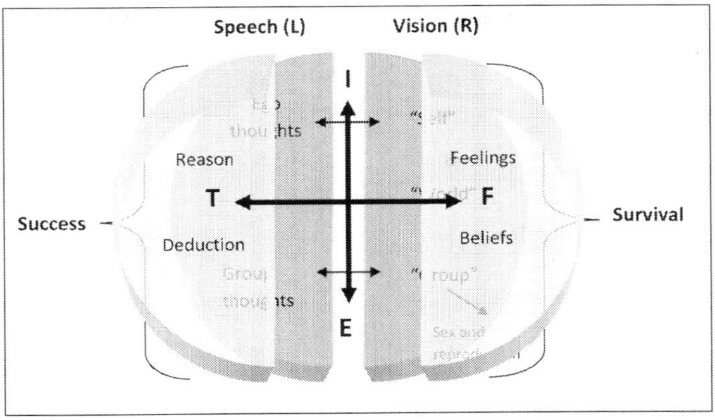

Figure 8. *The second Jungian axis of* ***T****hinking/****F****eeling is shown at a cognitive level above the base because it did not develop until Homo sapiens developed speech. This axis is also tested by the Myers-Briggs Type Indicator test.*

Sensing/Intuition comprise the third Jungian axis. These polar ends are described as:

- Sensing
    - Preference for obtaining information through the senses as facts and details
- INtuition
    - Preference for obtaining information as relationships, patterns, and possibilities

The S/N axis is added in Figure 9. Note that to model the S/N axis, higher levels of cognition are added. This is because this axis represents orientation to the base levels of sensations or to the higher cognitive levels. This Jungian axis was necessarily added after the first two axes. The first two axes were quite quickly (in evolutionary time frames) introduced with the development of vision and speech, respectively. This third axis has been under continual development since the second axis was established.

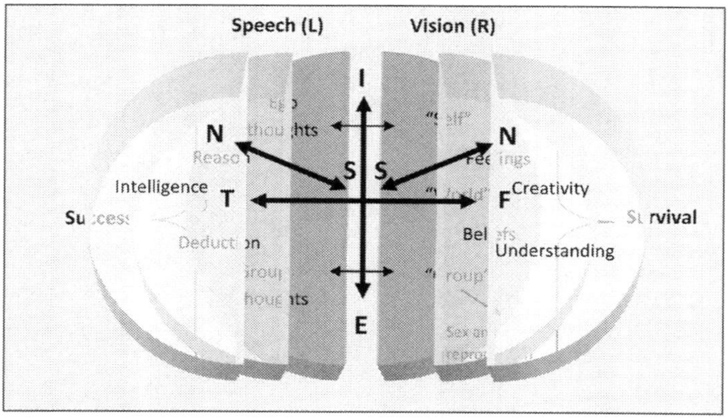

Figure 9. *The third Jungian axis represents orientation to the senses or the higher cognitive functions. It is likewise tested by Myers-Briggs.*

THE MYERS-BRIGGS TYPE INDICATOR TEST

The Myers-Briggs Type Indicator test was developed in 1962, the year after Carl Jung died, by the daughter/mother team of Isabel Myers and Katharine Briggs. It is a paper and pencil test with 93 forced-choice questions. Originally based on the Jung typologies, this test is very widely used for career counseling, team building, professional development, life coaching, and counseling among others.

Carl Jung never attempted to quantify his psychological types. His three bipolar axes result in a total of eight exclusive types: combinations of each pair. Myers and Briggs created and tested for a fourth axis called the "attitude scale" (**J**udging vs. **P**erceiving). Judging is a preference for a judging process for planning and organization whereas Perceiving is Preference for a perceiving process that is flexible and open to options.

The Carl Jung three axes are very consistent with the sensory mind. Further study may reveal whether/if the fourth axis added by Myers-Briggs has theoretical or functional value. Although the Myers-Briggs test is widely used and has been the subject of considerable inquiry, it is not yet clear whether the test is valid – i.e. does it really test what it proposes? Perhaps the Sensory Mind distinctions here can help to determine if it is a valid measure of the Jungian axes.

Sensory Mind Summary

The division of our brain and mind into a vision-based and a speech-based cognitive component is consistent with known evolutionary development of eyes and hearing/speech. The parallel-wired sense of vision and the sequential communication ability of speech serve as the base level neural circuitry from which our cognitive abilities developed. The dichotomy, which can be observed through introspection about our own consciousness, is also largely separated into the 2 cerebral hemispheres. This dichotomy is also consistent with some of the most influential writings and thinkers from history including the Story of Adam and Eve, the Greek philosophers, and Sigmund Freud and Carl Jung.

The vision-based mind is shared with the animals and contains all of the self-identity and group-identity information that comes from that world. It is a silent world insofar as there are no words. Thinking or reasoning do not occur in the right-brain mind. But, the right brain should not be diminished in its importance to our individual and collective life, as labels such as "dark", "sinister", "unconscious", etc. may imply. Our survival instincts come from that visual side. Likewise our concept of "self" resides in our vision-based mind. Also, our most basic drive for survival resides on the vision-based side and is driven by our "self" and "group" constructs. Vision-based cognition also drives our instincts for reproduction and sex.

Our speech-based left brain separated us from the animals and has served as the major basis for the amazing accomplishments of Homo sapiens at transcending other life forms on this planet.

Our concept of "group" (or "collective unconscious" in deference to Jung) and our "group thoughts" have provided the mental structure to enable us to organize our groups and civilizations from pre-history through early and current Civilizations. In this respect, the human mind is a collective event housed in all of our minds. As members of the same species, we genetically share most of the same anatomical and physiological aspects of the brain. It's as if we all have the same computer hardware and programs and are sharing files with one another.

The separation of our mind into vision-based and speech-based portions that have different cognitive modes can also apply to our historical development of groups and civilizations. The history of humans, told as the development of our collective right and left brains, will be told in the next sections.

CHAPTER 5

What Does This Mean to Human Behavior (ME)?

Our Consciousness

In this section we will use the Sensory Mind concept to investigate how it affects individual human behavior. You can apply it in the third person, or apply it to yourself.

Each of us has a consciousness that comes from our mind. Our entire life is experienced by our consciousness. Therefore, we effectively ARE our consciousness. Our consciousness, as discussed earlier, is comprised of our wordless feelings and emotions that come to us from the right-brain sense of "self" and also from our left-brain, word based, and thinking Ego that was added when we developed speech. This is shown in Figure 10.

Our consciousness is the way in which we experience life. We each have an individual consciousness that is a combination of our right-brain sense of "self" and our Ego that is the thinking left-brain correlate. The Ego generally overwhelms our sense of consciousness. The behavior motivators that come from the right brain and left brain (needs and desires respectively) are different and related to the respective survival and success objectives of the vision and speech based mind components.

The history of our species is, essentially, the history of the development of our left brain, and it has become highly developed. Related to that success, our Ego dominates our consciousness and who we think and believe we are as an individual. Many of us are even unable to introspectively appreciate the right brain contribution to consciousness. Many previous writers and scholars do not even include the right brain sense of "self" as part of our consciousness, relegating its contributions to our consciousness and self as "unconscious". However, the position taken here is that the wordless emotions and feelings that come to us from the right brain are a strong part of our consciousness and who we are as a person.

The deeply embedded objective of our right brain is survival, whereas the objective of our left brain has been success. As result, our behavior motivators from the right and left brain are different. "Needs" come from our right brain. "Desires" come from our left brain.

Our orientation to "self" or "group" (I/E)

The Self/Group Axis

The self/group axis is the oldest and most fundamental to human behavior. This comes to us from the very initial development of the vision system and its architecture as developed 570 million years ago in the Cambrian period. We share this axis with nearly all animals on the planet.

The distinction between self and group is fundamental to us and comes deep from the right brain. In our species, the distinction between self and group has become fairly intricate. Our right brain senses of "self" and 'group" have been significantly modified and complicated by the left brain "Ego" and "Group Think".

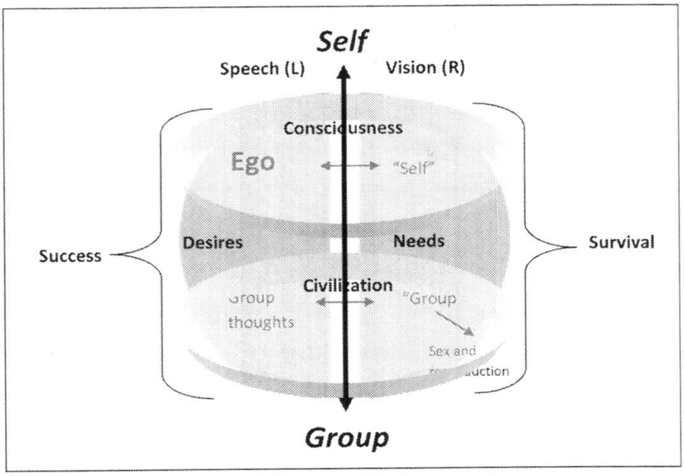

Figure 10. *The Self/Group axis is the oldest and most basic. This comes to us from the depths of our right brain, although the left brain has now played a significant role in this axis. This axis affects human behavior on a group and individual level more significantly than any other.*

SELF-DESIRES VS. GROUP-RESPONSIBILITIES

Self-desires emanate from the desires of our ego and the needs of our right-brain self. Our self-desires are very fundamental to each of us. Group-responsibility emanates from our group needs. Our sense of group-responsibility has always been part of human behavior and has its correlate in the animal world. Group responsibility plays a major role in the species drive for Darwinian survival. Our sense of group-responsibility is a fundamental part of what it is to be human, and a fundamental part of life.

> *Our self-desires and group-responsibilities broadly categorize the motivators of our individual behaviors. When behavior is motivated by self-desire, the benefits accrue directly to the individual. When behavior is motivated by group-responsibility, the benefits accrue directly to the group and indirectly to the individual. Ultimately, group success is what is important to species development and survival.*

Possibly the largest part of our individual human behavior and our needs is based upon our need to feel that we are contributing.

Viktor Frankl, author of *Man's Search for Meaning*, was a psychiatrist who survived Hitler's concentration camps and wrote observations of his fellow prisoners. These were people for whom life was reduced to almost nothing. Every material possession, every freedom, and nearly all hope had been taken from these prisoners. Their lives had been reduced to simple survival. He wrote, "A man who becomes conscious of the responsibility he bears toward a human being who affectionately waits for him, or to an unfinished work, will never be able to throw away his life. He knows the "why" for his existence, and will be able to bear almost any "how"." Our needs to contribute to others and also to feel needed by others are very close to our human core.

Most of us have a deeply seated inner NEED to contribute to the whole that comes to us from the right brain...and even deeper. This is our sense of group-responsibility. It is deeply seated in terms of the length of time from our early human emergence and in terms of depth within our human core. Our need for one another and what we each bring to one another by our bonding is central to our mind and to our species. There is a crying human need to help and contribute. Life is not full without it. When we work together to meet those needs, we can seemingly do anything. Civilization is the result.

GROUP–RESPONSIBILITY AND INDIVIDUAL SATISFACTION

Group-responsibility is an essential part of the human core. It certainly has been part of what it is to be human since the first small bands of humans huddled around a fire.

We obtain pleasures of the body and mind by satisfying our self-desires. The pleasures, or personal benefits, we receive from meeting our needs for group-responsibility are not as immediately evident.

When our behaviors are primarily motivated by our sense of group-responsibility, we are motivated by the needs of others, by the needs of the group, and according to the nobler principles of good morals and ethics.

Such actions are directed towards helping other people - such as spending the time to take them to the doctor, or helping someone paint their house. A scientist who discovers a new treatment for a disease will likely receive monetary rewards and hence satisfy self-desires. However, s/he will receive even greater self-satisfaction from knowing the contribution that the treatment makes to those in need and to civilization as a whole. This is the same satisfaction that an architect receives when the building is built or that a hairdresser receives when their customer is happy. Also, when we take the higher road in life, we feel good about it. The higher road is always the self-less one. It is the one that is according to the higher principles and morals of the group and that contributes to the good of the group.

Freud proposed that when actions of the ego violate principles and beliefs of the superego, the superego causes feelings of guilt and self-reproach - highly damaging and undesirable feelings. However, when the actions of the ego support the beliefs of the superego, then the superego rewards with feelings of great satisfaction. The rewards of superego satisfaction are different than the rewards from meeting the desires of the id.

Meeting the needs of our group-responsibility gives us great satisfaction. When we act in ways that are against our group-responsibility, it causes feelings of guilt and self-reproach.

Think of the satisfaction that you receive when you can bring a smile to someone's face because of an act of kindness. That satisfaction comes from our sense of responsibility to others. It is very self-satisfying because it is self-less. Think of the satisfaction that comes from doing a good job. These types of satisfaction are very different from the satisfaction that comes from meeting our self-desires.

We all certainly enjoy the satisfaction and pleasure that derive from meeting our self-desires. We enjoy going to the movies, driving a nice car, wearing nice clothes, traveling and going out to eat. We recognize these activities and commodities as being self-serving. We need not feel guilty about them – unless we experience them at the expense of others. They give us pleasure because it is pleasurable to meet our self-desires.

However, if our life consists entirely of meeting our self-desires, it feels empty. The activities and commodities that please our self-desires are those that money can buy. Although it is very nice to have money, money clearly does not buy happiness or true satisfaction with life. Money and the things that it buys to satisfy our self-desires cannot meet the greater satisfaction that comes from meeting our needs to contribute to the whole – our group-responsibility needs.

The key to individual happiness and self-satisfaction is fulfilling our deep inner need to contribute to the whole – i.e. fulfilling our group-responsibility.

Harold Kushner, author of *When All You've Ever Wanted Isn't Enough*, writes: "…the key to our happiness…is the sense that we are using our abilities, not wasting them, and that we are being appreciated for it." This is the fulfillment of our need to contribute to the whole – to make our civilization better for the fact that we were here. If we do so it satisfies us in ways that meeting our self-desires cannot.

When our behavior is motivated by our sense of group-responsibility, we are satisfying a need that is very close to the essence of life. This gives us great satisfaction, a type of satisfaction that transcends the pleasures of meeting our self-desires. We all have an internal need to satisfy our group responsibility, and meeting this need is what gives our life "meaning". It also gives each of us strong shoulders upon which others can stand.

This is the essence of building the strength of the group. It is also the essence of Darwinian survival.

Individual differences

The Self/Group axis bears many similarities to the Jungian Introvert/ Extravert axis. Carl Jung identified the I/E axis as the most fundamental to human behavior. This is also supported by the Sensory Mind theory offered herein. The Self/Group axis comes to our mind as one of the earliest concepts encoded by the sense of vision that has resulted in our right brain.

Actually, It is likely that the sense of self/group was part of life even before vision developed in the Cambrian period. Even the earliest animal species were comprised of individual organisms that survived as a group, or species. The differentiation between self and group almost certainly pre-dates vision. However, insofar as our human mind goes, the self/group differentiation primarily comes to us from the sense of vision and the cognitive skills built thereupon.

Some people are more oriented towards the group. They can be very giving towards others in terms of providing care, attention, services, etc. They can be considered "selfless". They are very good citizens of the group and great group members.

Others are more oriented towards the self. They are more prone to being loners and towards being into their self ("Selfish") than into looking after the needs of others. Such people tend to march to their own beat in life on paths separate from the group.

The above concepts are very similar to the extraversion/introversion differences noted by Carl Jung. He described the differences in terms of energy flow: an extravert's psychic energy flows outwards to others whereas an introvert's flows inward. Extraverts feel more energetic in a group whereas introverts feel more energetic when alone. Another way to characterize introvert/extravert is that introverts gravitate inward when dealing with important issues whereas extraverts gravitate towards talking with others.

> *The Self/Group axis seems very similar to the I/E axis as defined by Carl Jung, but also seems to differ somewhat from the colloquial uses of "introversion" and "extraversion". Common uses of both terms seem to most often refer to sociability which, although likely related to self/group leanings, can also be substantially different. Self/group refers to broader learnings and behavioral patterns. Those with a leaning towards self are better at self-expression in life and also towards satisfying self-desires. Those with a leaning towards group feel a stronger bond and responsibility towards the group. This difference can be very different than the presence or absence of good sociability skills.*

Sigmund Freud and self-group

This division into self-desire and group-responsibility has a correlate in the field of psychoanalysis. Sigmund Freud's (1856-1939) theory of psychoanalysis was largely based upon his observations of the development of personality and human behavior from birth, through infancy and childhood, and into adulthood. Based upon his observations he developed a structural model of mind development. His contributions are still foundational in psychoanalysis and have been very influential in our thoughts about the human mind.

Freud divided the mind into three hierarchical parts: the id, ego and superego (see Figure 5). As the baby emerges from the womb it has only very basic needs to eat, drink, defecate, urinate, stay warm, etc. These fundamental needs are requirements of the id – the needs of our right brain "self". The "pleasure principle" governs our behavior in meeting the needs of the id. The infant demands immediate gratification of the needs of the id.

On the other end of the hierarchy is the superego, which is our conscience and sense of morality. According to Freud the superego is part of the unconscious mind and is internalized in the child based upon their observations and experiences with others - beginning with their parents. The superego is our sense of what is right and wrong. The superego is essentially our sense of group.

The ego is our conscious, or left brain, self and governs our actions according to the "reality principle". The ego balances the needs of the id and the superego. As the child grows and develops the superego (sense of conscience and morality), it learns that pleasure satisfaction of the id must be tempered with judgment of what is right and wrong. Although pleasure satisfaction of the id would support crying behavior or taking merchandise from a store without paying for it, the superego understands that this is inappropriate. The ego, which governs conscious behavior, balances the needs of the id and superego. The superego enforces the rules of right and wrong upon the ego by causing feelings of guilt and self-reproach.

There are similarities between the Freudian model of development of the mind in a contemporary human and the model that results from the evolutionary development of the Sensory Mind presented herein. Behavior controlled by the Freudian id is very similar to that advocated as meeting the needs of the right brain self. The influence of the Freudian superego upon human behavior is very similar to the sense of group responsibility advocated herein. These similarities are not surprising because both models describe the same thing (the human mind); one uses the development of an individual person and the other uses the evolutionary development of *Homo sapiens.*

Our orientation to "thinking" or "feeling" (T/F)

Thinking/Feeling

The Thinking/Feeling axis was developed when we first acquired speech and developed cognition around its neural architecture. In fact, the human story is the story of the development of our species' left brain and its thinking role in self and group.

If the Self/Group axis is the strongest in terms of affecting mainstream human behavior and our group organizations, then the Thinking/Feeling axis affects our personal behavior and daily existence more than any other. We can sense the Thinking/Feeling in our own consciousness, since every part of the consciousness we can identify is experienced as a feeling or a thought. Feelings come to us from the silent world of the vision-based right brain, and thoughts come to us from the speech-based left brain.

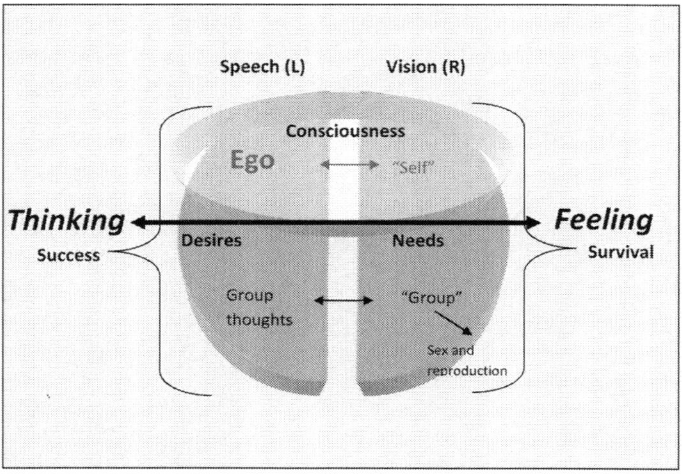

Figure 11. *The Thinking/Feeling axis was established when our species departed the animal world. Our consciousness is filled with Thinking and Feeling. Our daily living is experienced as thinking and feeling. Significant distinctions between individual humans exist along this axis.*

Our "silent" right brain has no words. However, it can very strongly exert its influence over our consciousness and our being. Our feelings and emotions sometimes overwhelm us. Emotions such as anger, love, being hurt, revenge, sorrow, elation, etc. can be extremely powerful. It is also difficult putting words to these emotions. Poets have attempted to do so, but almost always fall short of being able to perfectly describe an emotion.

Our Ego is our thinking self. For most people, the thinking ego dominates our consciousness. Our thinking ability is amazing. Consider all the thinking about things you are doing as you read this book. We can think about things far beyond the desires of our ego. We can think about our group responsibilities, what is right or wrong, and the meaning of life. We can even think about the feelings and emotions experienced by the right brain.

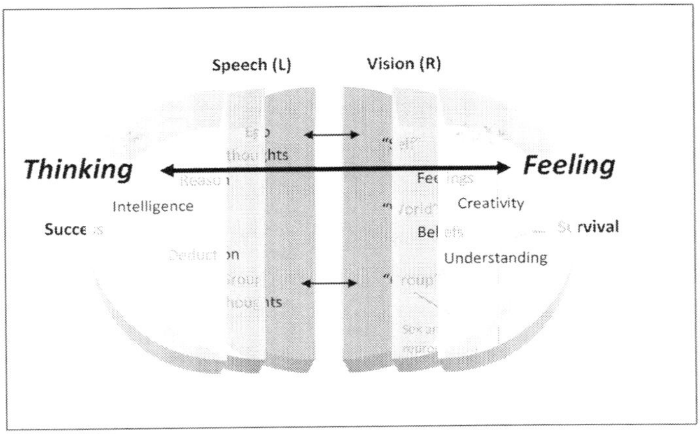

Figure 12. *Our right and left brains have developed higher-level cognitive skills based upon the senses of vision and speech respectively. These higher levels have added to the complexity of both thinking and feeling.*

People differ in their thinking/feeling weighting. Some people are much better in touch with their feelings, whereas, others seem remote from their feelings and live instead in the "rational" thinking left brain. Those who are in touch with their feelings are considered "sensitive"; those who are always rational can be considered cerebral but often can also appear insensitive and unfeeling. We can become "aware" of our feelings when our thinking left brain can verbalize or think about the fact that they are there. The feelings are word-less, but our thinking consciousness can "say" that they are there. We all have feelings, but some are more able to be aware of them than others. Sometimes we have a background feeling that is gnawing at us. We may not be aware of it, but it may eventually get the attention of our left brain and rise to "awareness".

There appears a wide range of human capacity for the left brain thinking to be aware of the right brain feelings and for it to motivate behavior. Some people are known to "wear their feelings on their sleeve". Such individuals are known to be very emotional. Others keep their emotions under strong control, with the rational left brain suppressing the emotional effects.

OUR ORIENTATION TO "SENSING" OR "INTUITION" (S/N)

SENSING/ INTUITION

Carl Jung introduced the sensing/intuition axis. As discussed earlier, this axis indicates orientation towards the senses (direct sensory input) or towards the higher cognitive functioning. This axis was also identified by Plato in the Divided Line. This axis is shown in the figure below.

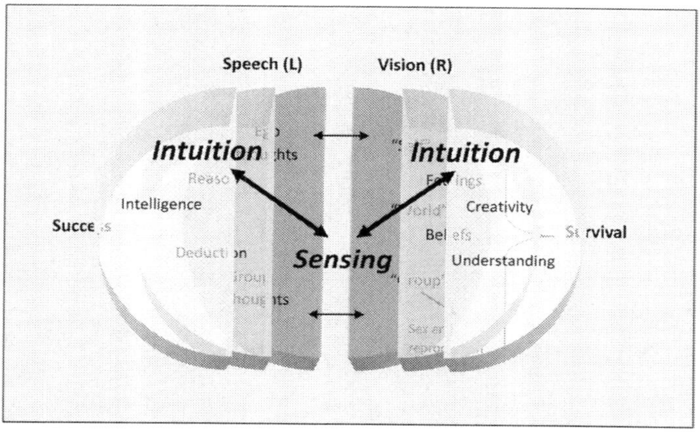

Figure 13. *The sensing/intuition axis was defined by Carl Jung. In the Sensory Mind model, this axis represents orientation to the senses (vision, hearing, and perhaps other senses) or towards the higher cognitive skills based upon them.*

A Sensor loves sensory stimulation. They enjoy activities that are sensory rich in the way they stimulate the body. They love going to movies – preferably those packed with action and sound. They seek sensory experiences like sports, outdoor activities, and the arts. They are more reactive and less contemplative.

An Intuitive is comfortable dealing with thoughts, ideas, and concepts. They can easily spend a lot of time in their head. As result, they are often comfortable being with themselves. They don't need a lot of outside stimulation in the form of people or things.

An Intuitive is good at putting ideas together in a structure. This is one of the highest levels of left/right brain synergy. The left brain is great at knowing facts and coming to deductions about them. But, it is an additional skill to be able to combine the facts in a meaningful way to support or create larger concepts that require right brain architecture.

"Listen to your intuition." Intuition is one of the highest uses of our mind. An intuition comes to us from the right brain. It is something that just "feels" good or right, or even bad or wrong. We "feel" intuition first. It has been something ruminating in the background. The right brain feeling has been informed by the left brain on many issues. The "feeling" that comes to you is already pretty smart. But, then, your left brain needs to be receptive to appreciating it and putting it into terms the left brain can understand – thoughts and words.

Animals have what we would call "intuition". They are very astute, visual observers of their environment. They are aware of just about everything in their surroundings and can become alert, frightened, comfortable, or inquisitive depending upon the entirety of the sensory stimuli they receive. Humans can likewise process information from many sources and feel an intuition about something. When we are in an outdoor environment, we can use input from all of our senses to give us a feeling about that environment. For example, a soft rustling of leaves in the top of the trees, with a cool wind, distant thunder and darkening skies tells us that a storm is coming and we should move towards shelter. Advanced animals likewise have this ability.

Humans can apply this same "intuition" at higher cognitive levels. We can be in a social environment and understand the mood of the room based upon lighting, sound, and level of conversation. It creates a feeling that is non-verbal. A "woman's intuition" is not magical. Her intuition is based upon real sensory input and facts/conclusions developed by her left brain. In many cases we will be unaware of all the input that goes into our feelings or intuition. In a business environment we are aware of the people in the room, how most of them think about the issues to be discussed, expressions on faces, and body language. Some of the "facts" about the environment have been previously determined by our left brain thinking about the situation. We might have a well-thought out plan for our presentation to the group, but in a discussion we must be spontaneous in our reactions. We will react to the entirety of the environment including people's expressions and reactions. We rely on our feelings and intuition for our final and expressed behaviors.

A person who is intuitive can also be creative. An intuitive is able to understand a fairly complex array of facts and situations and be able to develop a novel approach towards solving the problem or creating a solution to meet the needs of all constituents. This is a skill that we hope our leaders have, whether they lead small or large groups of people.

The "intuition" described above involves parallel processing of information from several different sources. This is clearly a right brain function. However, much of the information or conclusions that are fed into the intuitive right brain function come from left brain fact gathering and conclusions based upon reasoning. High left brain functioning involves being able to gather the correct facts and use reasoning to analyze them and come to conclusions based upon those facts. The addition of right brain intuition enables the person to assimilate facts and conclusions from several sources or areas of inquiry and create something new from them.

Our left brain is rational and logical and it very much runs like a digital or binary computer. Although both the right brain and left brains have higher levels, it is likely that the control of the highest level human functions come from the right brain – our intuition. Carl Jung described the intuitive in terms consistent with right brain function. He described intuition as being unconscious and bringing forth ideas and seeing possibilities in situations. Also, the common usage of intuition refers to non-verbal feelings and ideas that come to us. In the end, it is likely that the highest functioning of the human mind comes from the highest cognitive skills of our vision-based right brain.

CHAPTER 6

Early Humans – Emergence from Nature

God, Death, and Burials

As discussed in the first section, the vision-based concept of "group" was one of the earliest concepts formed as result of the sense of vision. "Group" has been part of animal life all the way back to the Cambrian period. Animals have historically grouped together within species and continue to do so. The grouping behavior is caused and mediated by the concept of group that is common to members of a species.

We (*Homo sapiens*) likewise have a vision-based concept of "group" that causes and enables us to instinctually group with one another. This is grounded in the vision-based animal world from which we came, and of which we remain a part. However, human grouping behavior has become extremely sophisticated in comparison to animal grouping because of our unique left-brain group thoughts. In fact, our left-brain abilities have enabled us to transcend, and even use for our benefit, all other life forms on this planet. "Survival", which is the Darwinian goal of the vision-based right brain, seems a distant concern of our current situation. The goal of the individual and collective left brain has become "Success". (see Figure

3) We first experienced such success in our early campfire groups when we accomplished enhanced security, cooked food, and made clothing. We currently experience success with televisions, electronic entertainment, travel, etc. The definition of "success" has varied across human groups and throughout human history.

The speech-based cognitive skills of the left brain have enabled us to dominate life on earth. Survival, the objective of the right-brain cognition has largely been assured. The objective of the individual and collective left brain is "Success" – as variously defined by human groups. In this section we will explore how development of our left brain concept of group, towards success, has led to the development of our current Civilizations.

GOD AND HOMO SAPIENS

Before we begin investigating the human story, however, the concept of god needs to be discussed. This is because god has been with us for a long time – probably back to the moment when we figuratively departed the Garden of Eden, or the relatively short period of time over which our speech-based mind allowed us to transcend the animal world.

The worship of a god and/or a belief system seems to be a major element in nearly all civilizations and in the earliest groups of man. Some of the very earliest cultural remains from our hunter/gatherer ancestors show belief in the supernatural. There is some evidence that Neanderthals and *Homo heidelbergensis* buried their dead and also participated in religious or mystical practices as long ago as 150,000-300,000 years. Worship appears simultaneously with the first evidence of human culture.

Early cave paintings show supernatural animals with mixed bodies, such as the head of a stag with large antlers, the face of an owl, ears of a wolf, arms with bear paws and tail of a horse. Burial sites show people buried with jewelry, food and statues of god-like figures. The god-like statuettes took several forms – men, women, animals, and mixtures. The provisioning for further living shows belief in life after death.

The form of god has varied throughout our history. The Egyptian Gods included animals and the sun, as well as deified Pharaohs. In many early societies, the individual who was head of the group was given the mantle of deity. The leader either WAS God, or had a presumed direct line of communication to God. This applied to many of the earlier large civilizations, such as the Aztec and Inca emperors, the Pharaohs in Egypt, and even extending to the emperor of Japan and kings and queens in more recent history.

The earlier forms of god were typically statues or similar physical objects. In either case the god-figure was a real object and people in the group could have access to the god – even if only from a viewing distance. As the groups became larger, bigger figures or symbols for god were required in order for people in the group to have access or view them. This required building large shrines such as the Egyptian pyramids or the Mayan temples. Invisible gods by-pass this problem of size and, therefore, can serve considerably larger groups of humans.

The concept of god appears to have been an integral part of humans from as far back in time as we can identify human culture; and it continues as a dominant part of the human condition today. The form of god can be very different in different human groupings. However, some groups, such as Buddhists, have a belief system which does not formally celebrate or believe in god.

Death and Human Burials

Besides stone tools, the earliest remains of human culture are graves. These earliest records of human burial show preternatural obsession with death and belief in a god. Burial was a very important step in becoming human, and it provides the earliest and most compelling evidence of our departure from the Garden of Eden.

> *Once we developed a "thinking" mind – and concurrently established the strong human ego, the ego started to take on a non-physical mantel. The ego seems not attached to the body. The ego fears death; and it also has a sense of immortality. This inevitably led to wonderment about what happened to the ego when the body dies. It also led to belief systems around death and preparation for an after-life.*

The very fact that early humans buried the dead body separated us from nature. Why would early humans go through the large effort of burying their dead? There was certainly no lack of easier places to put the body. Also, nature has a very parsimonious way of handling the remains of the dead – many animals and other organisms specialize in assuring that the remains are recycled.

Some animals will bury food, but animals do not bury their dead. Animals do not have a left-brain ego as do humans nor do they have a thinking consciousness. The most likely reason that humans bury their dead is the strong human ego that has developed along with our thinking ability. Burying protects the dead person's body from being devoured by scavengers.

The earliest humans knew that we each were different from nature around us. We had a thinking ego that gave us an identity that other beings in nature did not possess. Early humans also knew that their fellow humans had an ego. This is part of the strong connection that we feel with one another through our vision-based sense of "group". The living humans knew that the dead person had an ego similar to theirs and that the ego had been associated with the dead body. Where was the dead person's ego? There was no remaining evidence of the dead person's ego – could it still be somewhere in the dead body? If the body were preserved from nature's predators, would the dead person's ego be likewise preserved? We certainly hoped so - probably more for ourselves than for the dead person. More than likely, each living human knew that they did not want their body to be handled by nature - so they banded together to bury the dead body. We knew we were different.

What is it about being human, i.e. having an ego, that does not allow us to let nature handle our remains? The knowledge of death has come along with having an ego. This was the penalty imposed on humans when we were expelled from the Garden of Eden. Although some animals probably have a concept of death, they are unable to think about it. Certainly the animal concept of death is not nearly as well developed as ours. They fight for survival as an instinct, but because they don't have a thinking ego such as ours they are unable to think about death, unable to know that they will eventually die, and unable to worry about what it means.

Humans know about death, can think about it, don't understand it, and are terrified by it. Our ego feels so very real to us. It feels as if it exists outside of our body and almost has a life of its own. The ego is so real to us that we feel it must, in some way, be separate from the flesh and bones that constrain it. Our thinking ability cannot reconcile the strong sense of ego with the fact that there is no observable evidence that the ego continues after the body dies.

Some of the earliest records of human burials show that we went much farther than burying the dead – we also buried food along with the body and decorated the body with paint and jewelry. There are numerous indications of such ceremonies. This may have been a means of honoring the person. Perhaps we buried the person because of our strong human bond with that person and we buried their body because of respect. However, including food and other provisions in the burial site indicates the reason for burial is probably much deeper than this. The concept of an eternal ego that continues beyond death of the body is both comforting and compelling. Early humans apparently thought the body must be provisioned so that it could, in some way, support the continuation of the ego after death of the body. As civilization developed, these practices became ever more elaborate – resulting in mummification and building true wonders of the world such as the Egyptian pyramids.

Throughout human history there have been numerous different gods and religions. A major component of nearly all gods and religions has been to deal with the fact that our ego cannot believe that it dies with the body*. Religions give us a framework by which we can *believe* that the ego continues as a soul after the body dies. This concept is a fundamental part of nearly all religions.

---

* It must be noted that the teachings of Buddha are different in this respect. Buddhist teachings recognize the death of individuals and do not suggest a continuation of the individual ego as a soul. Such differences in civilizations will be discussed later.

We really don't know what happens after death. Our ego is so strong and palpable to us that we simply cannot accept it dies with the body. Therefore we have buried our dead along with religious worship that comforts us about our continuation. However, there is no observable evidence of a continuation of the ego.

God, Religion and the Sensory Mind

There is no evidence to indicate that animals believe in god. In the animal world of nature, life just IS. The world just IS. There are no words; hence, there are no questions and no need for answers. Animals strive to survive and they have the concepts of "self" and "group" and "world". However, in the wordless animal world, the state of the world is simply accepted and not questioned. There are no thoughts to question the world around them. They can't think about god.

There is some indication that animals have amazement or awe about the world around them. Monkeys have been observed to sit and watch a sunset - an indication of appreciation of beauty in the environment. Higher forms of animals certainly have advanced cognitive skills based upon the sense of vision. They are continuously immersed in the "world" of nature and very attuned to it with their non-verbal cognition. Elements in the world can almost certainly frighten, scare, soothe, entice, excite, or mislead them. They almost certainly have a strong appreciation for nature since they are immersed in it; but they also do not have the cognitive tools to ask questions about the world.

The concept of god appears to be uniquely human. The introduction of speech and associated verbally-based cognitive skills has enabled humans to formulate questions. The most amazing and fundamental unknown around us is the "world" – something that is fundamentally deep within our vision-based cognition. In the Cambrian period, the sense of vision provided for the concepts of "self", "group", and "world". The concept of the "world" is embedded in the cognition that developed from the sense of vision.

Belief in god apparently developed simultaneously with the development of our speech-based brain. As shown in the diagram of the Sensory Mind, god and religion explain the vision-based "world" to us. The concept of "god" is so fundamental to the human mind that it is shown to occupy a space between the right and left brains.

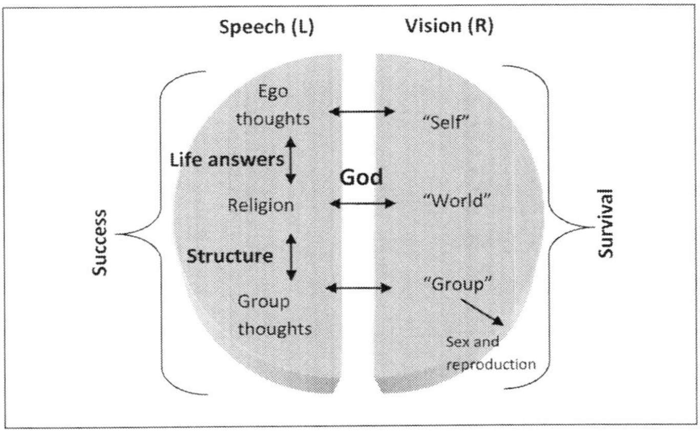

Figure 14. *The concept of god is based upon our left brain questioning about the many unknowns in the right brain concept of "world". The god concept is tied to some of the fundamental and earliest cognitive concepts in both the left and right brains. Religion is the set of left brain rules that are tied to belief in god.*

Because of our ego, our separation from nature, and our thinking ability, we have an immense number of questions about the unknown – especially questions concerning the meanings of life and death. The world is bewildering to us and our fundamental questions about it seem unanswerable. Belief in god provides answers and/or beliefs about the "world". The human concept of god has roots in both the vision- and speech-based cognition. The concept of "world" is embedded very deeply in the vision-based right brain; and the questions, answers, and god concept are likewise embedded in the earliest parts of our speech-based left brain.

The concept of god is deep and fundamental to both sides of our mind. It is tied to some of the earliest cognitive concepts of both the vision- and speech-based cognitions.

This also addresses our fear of dying. Our concept of ego is so strong that we cannot imagine it dies with the body. God and religion have given us belief systems to explain the unknown and to explain death to us. This was a very early concept in our evolutional development.

Religion gives us answers about the meaning of life and gives us comfort about dying.

Because of our strong sense of "group", we bond together with other humans and need rules to govern the inter-relationships. God and religion have also met this need. At first, such rules were relatively simple such as do not harm others and do not take from others. It is likely that one of the earliest tenets of religious teaching was what has commonly become known as the Golden Rule - "Do unto others as you would have done unto yourself." This forms the very basis for the development of cooperative living. The Code of Hammurabi, "an eye for an eye and a tooth for a tooth", is closely related to the Golden Rule - but stated in the negative. If you do wrong to someone, then equal wrong should be done to you.

As the size of human groups grew, especially with development of agricultural communities, the role of the gods also needed to grow. Larger groups of people occupying greater land areas require more intricate forms of organization and leadership. Larger groups require greater sophistication of structure. This includes a system of justice and some form of hierarchy to lead the group, as well as provision for meeting the economic needs of the hierarchy and the costs of managing the group. Taxation of some sort has likely been with us since the earliest days of agriculture - or even earlier. The role of god and religion expanded to meet the larger organizational needs of the larger human groups.

Religion has historically played the major role in managing groups of people. The primary practical and observable group function of religion has been to provide the shared ethics, morality, justice and rule by which members of the community interact.

Religion, group management, and group leadership have been intertwined throughout human history. This is a very efficient system. Religion provides answers about life and death to satisfy fundamental questions of each individual (ego); and religion also serves as the set of ethics, principals, and even operating procedures that guide the society. The leader of the society has often also been the leader of the religion.

Religions are much more than belief in a god. Throughout human history religions have met two basic human needs:

- Religions have provided answers about the meaning of life and death.
- Religions have provided social, economic, and political rules that manage, guide and lead groups of people.

In our current advanced civilizations, science has become our tool for investigating the world around us and explaining the unknown. No wonder there is a continual friction between religion and science; in some respects they have the same objective: to describe the "world".

"Religion is regarded by the common people as true, by the wise as false, and by rulers as convenient." Seneca the Younger, Roman philosopher, (3 B.C.-65 A.D.)

Early Human Development

Human history is largely a story of advancements in our verbal-based cognitive skills. The advancements in human groups and civilizations chronicle developments in "group-think". As a correlate, this suggests that the human mind (especially the verbal-based mind) was not as well developed earlier in history as it is now. Although this makes perfect sense from a developmental point of view, it is sometimes difficult to realize that the human mind was not always what it is today.

The World from which we emerged

We emerged from an animal world in which cognition was dominated by the sense of vision. Every advanced animal had a concept of "self" vs. "world", and "group" vs. "other". All creatures had self-awareness and were driven to survive. Survival involved reproduction.

Our earliest ancestors were not very distinct from the animals around them. Behavioral patterns were already deeply ingrained, and were consistent with behavior patterns in the animal world around them.

Animals clearly group with one another, as do humans. Advanced animals also demonstrate special behaviors and apparent feeling and emotions towards family members. Humans obviously have these behaviors. Many animals show herding behavior. Humans also display a type of herding behavior in terms of our propensity to congregate in groups - both small and large.

Dominance hierarchy is another attribute that is common to groupings of most advanced animals. Dominance is usually asserted by the strongest member of the group with a pecking order down through the ranks. Such hierarchies often provide reproduction, feeding, or other advantages to the dominant members of the group; thereby, encouraging favorable selection and evolution. Even in today's societies we observe dominance hierarchies. In fact, dominance hierarchies seem a necessary part of group management, whether animal or human.

> *Human group instincts and basic human group models came from the animal world from which we emerged. Humans came from the animal world and adopted the behavior models practiced in the animal world. These were the models upon which early human groupings and early human civilizations were based.*

EARLY HUMAN GROUPING

We also have some of the hunter and the hunted in our genes. We have conquered both by using our thinking. We domesticated most of the hunted (cattle, pigs, sheep) and some of the hunters (dogs and cats). As expert hunters we continued to hunt most large animals, often to extinction.

We *Homo sapiens* existed as hunter-gatherers until the beginning of agriculture 9,000-10,000 BCE. Prior to that time we lived in small groups without permanent shelter (other than a cave) and in nomadic search of food.

Archaeological evidence suggests that some of the very earliest burials, art, and evidence of belief in gods may have occurred as long ago as 100,000 years. However, culture in *Homo sapiens* flowered during a period of 60,000 to 30,000 years ago. Art and hard evidence of religions appear widespread near the latter part of that period. This is also the period of time during which items of personal decoration such as beads, pendants and perforated animal teeth are found. The wearing of personal items such as these shows a sense of personal identity. During this period of time, it is very clear that human behavior is distinguished from that of animals. We must certainly be speaking and thinking during this period of time.

At about this same time (60,000 to 30,000 years ago), tools become more complex and the hunting habits of humans changed quite significantly. Early humans were still hunter/gatherers during this period of time. They subsisted by hunting animals for food and clothing and picked food from the plant world as it was naturally available around them. Humans are also eating and hunting ibex and seals–animals that require considerable planning and coordination to locate and kill. Steven Mithen, author of *The Prehistory of the Mind – the Cognitive Origins of Art and Science*, suggests that our ability to anthropomorphize animals, i.e., attribute human thinking and characteristics to the ways in which animals behave, allowed us to predict animal behaviors and was extremely valuable in hunting.

It is also at approximately this same time that elaborate burials are found. These burials include clothing, food, and thousands of beads. Why would early humans be decorated so much in burial? The most logical reason is that they were being prepared for an after-life. The earliest artistic remnants from our history show religions and belief in gods.

"Self" and "Group" in Early Human Grouping

Our Homo ancestors, including *Homo Erectus*, Neanderthal (*Homo neanderthalensis)*, and early *Homo sapiens*, were hunter-gatherers. We lived in small groups, and each group had to totally provide for itself. Considerable cooperation was required to provide protection and sustenance for the group and its propagation. We needed one another for protection and survival. This sense of community originated from our vision-based cognition coming from the world of animals. Each individual had a right-brain feeling of "group", shared with other humans, that was tied to the survival instinct embedded in the right brain. However, we also knew that both individually and collectively we were different from the other animals around us. We had separated ourselves from nature with our left brain thinking - both as individuals and as groups. We became reliant upon one another. We also knew or sensed that we had mental prowess that exceeded any that existed elsewhere in the animal world - a world from which we were inherently different. Collectively, we were much stronger than we were individually.

In those early days, we were surrounded by a harsh and dangerous world. Commitment to the group was strong and emanated from the right-brain sense of "self" within ourselves. Survival of each human and their individual ego was dependent on the group. Individuals within the group began to acquire knowledge or skills that could benefit the group. This information was shared with others and became part of the verbally-based "group-think" that was overlaid on the right brain sense of "group" that is a fundamental part of human and animal cognition. Some humans became more skilled at hunting, others at food preparation, child rearing, or jewelry making. A group identity developed and each human felt commitment to the group.

The early "group-think", or the collective knowledge base of humans, was considerably less than today. The collective knowledge, or at least portions of it, became the common knowledge of all humans. It becomes part of the base knowledge that we are taught as children. Each individual might not know everything in the collective data base, but today we can Google it. We can easily see the advance of the collective knowledge base even within the span of one or two current generations–today's children are considerably more knowledgeable than we were at their age. This is because the knowledge developed and acquired by each generation is added to the collective database that is passed along to the next.

CHAPTER 7

Early Human History

Up to 12,000 years ago

Early African roots

We first appeared, in Africa, approximately 200,000 years ago. The earliest history of *Homo sapiens* is sketchy and it appears that the human mind was not well-developed in the earliest part of our existence. Signs of culture and burials only began to appear 100,000 years ago, and even then most of the cultural growth flowered 60,000 to 30,000 years ago. We did not migrate out of Africa until about 70,000 to 50,000 years ago. A lot seems to have happened in a relatively short span from 100,000 to 50,000 years ago. If I had to pick a time when Homo became human, I would pick that era.

Much of our existence in Africa was challenged by climate. An indication of the types of climate changes is the finding that 13,000 years ago the Sahara desert was actually a swamp and jungle. The Sahara is on a 20,000 year cycle in which it switches back and forth from desert to jungle. (This cycle is suspiciously close to the 26,000 year cycle during which the axis of the Earth's rotation, which wobbles like a top, circumscribes a circle in the heavens that encompasses three stars – the current North Star being Polaris.) There were considerable climate changes in Africa during our development there. It is likely that our adaptability, which emanates from our mind, enabled us to be successful in those changing climates. The reverse is also probably true, the changing climate nurtured evolution of advanced cognition.

OUT OF AFRICA

All waves of human development have come out of Africa. DNA analysis has enabled us to study our lineage. Mitochondrial DNA has been particularly valuable in looking at the X chromosome that is unpaired in males. Because it is unpaired, genetic variations in that part of the chromosome remain in male lineage and serve as markers that can be used to trace lineage. The oldest people in terms of being closest to the original genes have the greatest DNA variability. The San bush people in Africa are the oldest genetic people as determined with genetic marking. Even today the Sans bushmen language also has clicks in it; perhaps coming directly from the animal world? No other human language has such clicks. The genetic evidence indicates that we all trace our ancestral roots to a very small group of people in northeastern Africa, perhaps only 600 people (Wells, 2003), lending strength to the concept of Adam and Eve.

We migrated from Africa somewhere between 70,000 and 50,000 years ago. This is the same time during which there is growing evidence of our art, culture, and burials. The climate conditions in Africa were difficult at the time–likely prompting our exploration. Our adaptability, fueled by our growing cognitive skills, enabled us to spread quickly and widely.

As we moved into Asia, we must have encountered *Homo heidelbergensis* and Neanderthals, the latter of which do not disappear from the fossil record until only 28,000 years ago. The Neanderthal genome has been mapped, and there is no evidence of inter-breeding (Wells, 2003). It is interesting to surmise the interactions that occurred between these

Homo species. Our war-like history with one another suggests we may not have been kind to our inferiors. Obviously we survived and they did not; intelligence won the survival game. As one example, *Homo sapiens* developed projectile weapons whereas Neanderthals had only hand weapons. Many Neanderthal remains show many broken bones – likely because they needed to get closer to their prey. We could go after more game more safely.

The first migration from Africa was around the southern shores of the Arabian Peninsula and down the coast of India to the Kerala area on the western tip of South India, about 70,000 to 50,000 years ago. The oldest genetic person outside of Africa has been found in Kerala (Woods, 2003). In neighboring Tamil Nadu, geneticists testing DNA of local peoples have found genes from 50-60,000 years ago. In Kerala there are ancient Brahman chants, or mantras, that appear to be unrelated to any known language (Woods, 2003). These chants have been passed down for centuries–precisely sounded and taught from one generation to another. They have patterns but no known meaning. The sounds and rhythms have been related to birds, perhaps from a time when our speech patterns evolved from animal sounds.

From South India the migration path continued along the southern shoreline of Asia, arriving in Australia sometime between 60,000 and 46,000 years ago. The 150 miles of water between Asia and Australia may have been crossed by boat, or perhaps the ice age had lowered the oceans to create a land bridge.

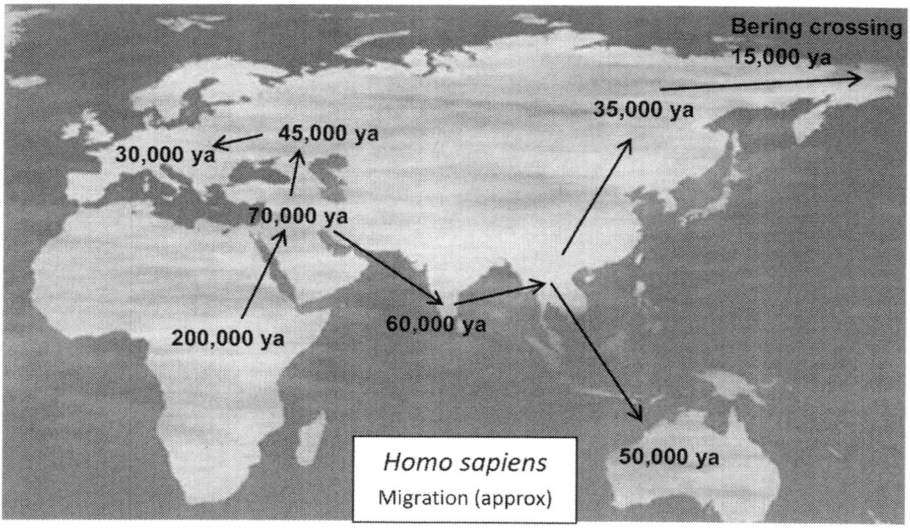

Figure 15. *Our major migration paths out of Africa. Dates (ya = years ago) are approximations,*

About 45,000 years ago a second group migrated from Africa up into the Middle East, and from there into central Asia. We were establishing ourselves in the Middle East and Asia, but there was no trace of humans in Europe. It took another 10,000 years for humans to arrive in Europe. The ancestors of the Europeans came from Central Asia (current Kazakhstan)– not directly from the Middle East. Europe was experiencing the Ice Age much worse than in the Middle East, making it more difficult to settle. Cave drawings in southern France from 30,000 years ago show the Ice age mammoths and such. Early European ancestors mostly lived in caves for protection from the climate. It is likely that in caves we evolved lower skin melanin in order to let through enough UV to create vitamin D - hence developing lighter skin color. Evolution works quickly.

There is evidence that human big game hunters arrived in northeast Asia (Siberia) around 35,000 to 30,000 years ago. This area was apparently settled from the south and also from the west. About 15,000 years ago we migrated to the Americas, almost certainly crossing the Bering Sea on a land bridge created by the lower ocean levels associated with an ice age.

We arrived in current day US about 13,000 years ago. Within 800 years of first arriving in North America, we had also peopled South America.

Human status, 12,000 years ago

By 12,000 years ago, we had largely populated our planet. Because of our adaptability and intelligence, we had become the dominant species on our planet, most likely hunting many other animal species into extinction. It has been estimated there may have been as many as 5,000,000 people on the planet at that time. For the first time in four billion years of life on this planet, a single species dominated the planet.

We were excellent at conquering and dominating the animal world. This is demonstrated by the fact that we drove to extinction many of the major land mammals in existence during our rise to the pinnacle of life on the planet. North America might be the best example of our ability to conquer and drive other animals into extinction. We arrived in the US about 13,000 years ago. Also 13,000 years ago the following major North American mammals were seen for the last time on Earth: Dire Wolf, Smilodon, Cave Lion, Giant beaver, Ground sloth, Mammoth, American Mastodon, American Camel, American Equine, and American lion (Wikipedia, 2011). These species disappear from the fossil records at about the same time that humans arrived.

Evolution has continued during the years of our dispersion around the planet. Evidence of this is seen by the regional characteristics that *Homo sapiens* have developed – resulting in the racial differences in appearance we can observe today. Once we had peopled the planet, large migrations were unlikely and Boeing 747's had not yet been invented….resulting in considerable localized in-breeding that nurtured localized evolutionary branches.

However, even though we had attained the dominant life position on this planet, we were still hunter gatherers. We had not yet controlled the plant world with agriculture, and there is no evidence of permanent dwellings other than caves. We were still largely nomadic and apparently lived in small groups - perhaps as tribes. Each small group of people had no concept of the size of the world, nor knowledge of other groups except for those with whom they came in direct contact.

We had conquered the planet, but our groups were likely still structured using animal group models such as dominance hierarchy, herding, and family. Our group-think abilities had enabled us to cooperate with one another in small groups. This cooperation and group intelligence made us the best hunters and we had almost certainly attained some forms of specialization for small-group efficiency. However, our group-think abilities had not yet enabled us to harness nature or to structure larger groups. Humankind was still living in an animal world.

Our sense of group was very strong. We felt strong kinship within the group, but probably did not feel kinship with any being outside of the group–including other *Homo sapiens.* We almost certainly felt no kinship with earlier homo species versions from which we came. For example, did *Homo erectus* feel kinship with Lucy? Did we feel any kinship with *Homo erectus* or *Neanderthal*? The record cannot support that and indicates the opposite. We probably drove earlier *Homo* species into extinction, the same way we did to many species of large animals. Our species, as a whole, operates by Darwinian rules.

How did we behave during this time? Were we parsimonious in terms of taking only that which we needed? The horizons probably seemed limitless, and when we conquered one location and stripped it of animal and plant resources, we moved on. The world seemed infinite in size. The result was sort of an unintended scorched earth policy.

Were there any conversations about the morality, or long term effects? I doubt it; our communication probably only extended to the nearby human groups and not much beyond. We had no concept of the size of the world; writing had not yet been invented to enable widespread communication.

How did we behave towards one another? We were still hunter-gatherers and our groups were still probably quite small and limited to bands of people. Towns, villages, and cities were not yet developed and we were still largely cave dwellers. Did we cooperate with neighboring bands, or, did competition drive us to conflict with one another? Almost certainly both kinds of behavior occurred; unfortunately, recorded history of more recent times suggests conflict may have been very common. Base human behavior appears to be aggressive between groups.

> *It took us only about 50,000 years to populate and dominate the planet after leaving Africa. It has taken us only an additional 12,000 years to attain our current status on this planet.*

PRE-CIVILIZATION PERIOD

AGRICULTURE AND ANIMAL DOMESTICATION

A transcendent step in our development occurred when we discovered the ability to control plant and animal life – i.e. the beginning of agriculture in 10,000 to 9,000 BCE.[1] Archaeological evidence indicates that agriculture and animal domestication revolutions seemed to occur independently in at least seven different locations. This revolution occurred very shortly after we had conquered the planet. Perhaps these revolutions were an obvious solution for the growing populations of people and the finite and limited sources of naturally growing food. Even though agriculture may have been an obvious solution to the growing populations and limited food resources, it is interesting that it occurred independently in several locations. This indicates a strong commonality of abilities and reactions across different human groups. However, it must also be pointed out that strong human grouping behavior, mixed with our inter-group aggression behavior (we are, unfortunately, very war-like), would have caused agriculture to spread to neighboring groups very quickly.

> *"And Adam knew Eve his wife; and she conceived, and bare Cain, and said, I have gotten a man from the Lord.*
>
> *And she again bare his brother Abel. And Abel was a keeper of sheep, but Cain was a tiller of the ground." Genesis 4: 1-2.*

1 Please note that we now shift from "years ago" to "BCE". (12,000 years ago is nearly the same as 10,000 BCE). The invention of agriculture seems an appropriate milestone at which to make this change.

How interesting that the two sons of Adam and Eve separately domesticated plants and animals.

No longer were we dependent upon gathering food that grew in the wild – as do other foraging animals. We domesticated animals and could use them for food and clothing. We learned to control plants, selecting seeds and planting them in locations where we knew they would grow. We harvested the plants and stored the harvest for future times when we knew food would be scarcer. However, when we planted, we also needed to be in the same area when the harvest was ready. We began to develop permanent living places and no longer were nomadic. Our left-brain "groupthink" was serving us well.

As we developed from small bands of hunter gathers to larger agriculture-based communities our group dependence and individual commitment to the community also grew. Greater individual specialization was required. Food became more plentiful; and with considerably less community time spent to obtain it. More time could be spent in making shelters against the elements, putting up fences, making jewelry, making clothes, making pottery, making furniture, etc. We grew evermore dependent upon one another. Each individual and their ego became increasingly dependent upon the success of the group because we each became less able to do everything that was needed for our own individual survival. Success of the group was not only important to the survival of each individual, but to the quality of life of each individual as well, which in turn was also intimately tied to the collective contributions of each member of the group.

Community growth could not have occurred if individuals were solely motivated by meeting the needs of their ego. As human communities grew in complexity, the relationships and community "rules" that governed meeting "self" vs. "group" needs also needed definition.

The smaller agricultural communities grew in numbers and in complexity during the centuries. Agriculture, one of our first sciences, became more sophisticated as we began to learn more about the needs of plant life. We discovered which seeds to select, when to plant, how to select the proper soil conditions, how to use hand drawn and then irrigated water – all to obtain optimal growth. With application of these techniques, the food supply quickly doubled, then doubled, then doubled again – similar to other "technology revolutions" we have had.

The spread of agriculture - 10,000 BCE to 5,000 BCE

The developments of agriculture and animal domestication began our transition from hunter-gatherers who were living among the animals to town and city dwellers. We became freed from the constant demands of foraging for food. We could establish permanent living communities where we felt collective safety from predators. We now had placed another level of separation between ourselves and the animal world around us.

Although agriculture appeared independently in several areas of the world, it first appeared in the Fertile Crescent, apparently nurtured by the Mediterranean climate. Larger numbers of humans began to live with one another. The first communities or small towns formed around 6,000 to 5,000 BCE. Approximately 10,000 people lived in the Tigris, Euphrates, and Nile communities by 5,000 BCE. The region between the Tigris and Euphrates rivers, in current day Iraq, has been referred to as Mesopotamia, the Greek for "between rivers".

Early cities

The earliest settlements of people began about 7,000 BCE and grew into villages. The earliest cities appeared in Mesopotamia around 4000 BCE. Uruk, in current Iraq, is often considered the world's first city. Cities, of course, were enabled because we had discovered agriculture. All of this time, we are growing in our group-think abilities while our populations are also growing. Without any more predators around, our rate of reproduction climbed quickly.

By the late 4th millennium BCE, the Mesopotamian area was divided by about a dozen independent city-states. Each city had a temple at its center that was dedicated to and celebrated the particular patron God or Goddess of that city. Each city also had a king or ruler who was closely associated with the God or Goddess. The temples were the most dominant and important building of each city. They were built to be visible from long distances.

These cities were the largest groups of people at the time. The group organization was largely a dominance hierarchy with the God or Goddess at the center of the group. This group organization was nearly the same as campfire group organization around the image of a god. The larger group simply required a larger physical symbol around which to congregate.

Each early city had its own God or Goddess, which occupied the center of the city. Our group organization was centered on a God as the leader.

Status – 3250 BCE

Our group-think had enabled us to bond together in larger, agriculturally-based communities. Each community was likely organized as a dominance hierarchy and based on a theocracy. God was leading, and we were organized on this planet like a bunch of ant hills. We also had just discovered writing for broader communication with one another, and had discovered the group-think ability of conceiving a universal god. The stage was now set for our group-think to expand to the next level: civilizations.

Self and Group in Early History

As discussed earlier, the vision-based concept of "group" was one of the earliest concepts formed as a result of the sense of vision. "Group" has been part of animal life all the way back to the Cambrian period. Animals have historically grouped together within-species and continue to do so. The grouping behavior is caused and mediated by the concept of group that is common to members of a species.

We (*Homo sapiens*) likewise have a vision-based concept of "group" that causes and enables us to instinctively group with one another. This has come to us from the vision-based animal world from which we came, and of which we remain a part. However, human grouping behavior has become extremely sophisticated in comparison to animal grouping because of our unique left-brain group thoughts. In fact, our left brain abilities have enabled us to transcend, and even use for our benefit, all other life forms on this planet. "Survival", which is the Darwinian goal of the vision-based right brain, seems a distant concern of our current situation. The goal of the individual and collective left brain has become "Success". We first experienced such success in our early campfire groups when we experienced enhanced security, love and compassion, and clothing. We currently experience success with televisions, electronic entertainment, travel, homes, cars, career, etc. The definition of "success" has varied across human groups and throughout human history.

Writing - Linking Vision and Speech

Writing

Writing was quite an amazing part of the development of our mind. Writing became the strongest tie between vision and speech. At its essence, writing is the pictorial (vision and right brain) representation of speech (left brain).

An interesting thing about writing is that it seemed to occur independently and nearly simultaneously in several areas of the world. It is highly likely that our mind skills were similar or the same throughout the world, and that the living situation of our species was likewise similar – thereby resulting in similar accomplishments and timelines. This seemed to be the case with the development of agriculture and also with the development of writing.

The very earliest forms of writing are considered proto-writing– because they are essentially pictographs, or drawings of things such as sheaves of wheat. Such proto-writing has been documented as early as 6600 BCE in China (Jiahu Script) and 5300 BCE in Southeastern Europe (Vin□ a script). However, this pictorial representation of objects does not really qualify as writing. Perhaps words, verbally spoken, became associated with those pictures. However, the pictures, by themselves, do not carry phonetic information. This does not really meet our commonly recognized concept of writing.

True writing, or phonetic writing, seemed to develop in several locations at nearly the same time – about 3400-3200 BCE. This occurred in Sumeria, Egypt, India, and China. These were languages in which pictures, or characters, represented sounds that could be pieced together in various combinations to represent speech patterns from which words are made. The first forms of writing seemed more functional than literate; i.e. they were lists or short communications. They did not capture a story or have a larger message to them.

EARLIEST LITERATURE

The first literature is not until 600-1,000 years after the first writing appeared. The earliest literature goes back to about 2,500 to 2,200 BCE. This is really the first time that we are able to get inside the minds of the writers. The earliest literature also already hints at differences in attitudes in people from different areas. Not surprisingly, many of the earliest pieces of literature that have come down to us are about god and about wars.

THE BIBLE

The first five books of the Old Testament are attributed to Moses, who lived approximately 1500-1300 BCE. Many of the events, such as the creation story and the flood, occurred well before Moses; therefore, he recorded stories that lived in the oral tradition at the time. Apparently we were telling stories that were known by fairly large populations even before we were able to write them.

THE EPIC OF GILGAMESH

This epic tale of the King of Uruk (the first city) and his wild, untamed friend comes from Mesopotamia. The oldest known writings of this piece of literature date to about 700 BCE, however the story is believed to be centered on a time approximately 2700 BCE. For 2,000 years it existed in oral tradition or in earlier written forms that are no longer available or not yet discovered.

The Iliad and the Odyssey

Homer, who is credited with writing the *Iliad* and the *Odyssey*, along with other Homeric poems, probably lived around 850 BCE. However, the Trojan War, of which he wrote, likely occurred in approximately 1180 BCE. This classic Greek story about the Trojan War began when Paris of Troy took Helen from her husband, Menelaus, who was the King of Troy. The story includes many gods, a war, and deception in war. This story seems to have set the tone, or recorded the existing tone, of the Greeks at the time. It seems a base from which sprang the Greek miracle beginning about 500 BCE.

The Vedas

The Vedas are the earliest literature, written in Sanskrit, which comes from the northern Indian sub-continent. They date from approximately 1700-1100 BCE. They are a collection of verses, some of which are still recited today as part of religious ceremonies. The Vedas contain mythological and poetic accounts of the formation of the world and have many prayers for life in general.

"Veda" is derived from the Sanskrit word meaning "to know". The Vedas are considered words of wisdom and truth. The Vedas have had a very large influence on the culture and beliefs on the Indian sub-continent. The Vedas likely represent the beliefs of the peoples of that time and location, and those beliefs serve as the foundation for the current Hindu and neighboring cultures.

A strong part of Hindu belief systems is that we can "know" the truth through self-reflection. By contrast, Western Christian culture has taught that we can only know the truth through belief in God.

The Mahabharata

This is a large epic tale that contains approximately 100,000 verses. The oldest forms of this text date to about 400 BCE, however a major portion of this epic is about a large war that occurred around 3,000

BCE. However, considerable debate about authorship, dates, and events contained in the Mahabharata continues.

This book of verses was written in Sanskrit and is foundational to Hinduism in India. It contains many philosophical discussions, including the four "goals of life" which are dharma (right action), artha (purpose), kama (pleasure), and moksha (liberation).

I Ching

The earliest known versions of this text are from about 400 BCE, however the writings seems to come from an era approximately 2800 BCE. The writings of the I Ching have been very influential in the Chinese culture.

Early literature summary

These, and other early writings, have had very large influences on the thinking of large groups of people. In most cases, the true authors of these documents are unknown, and they are often apparently written by several contributors. They likely represent the developing culture and belief systems of the peoples from which they came. It is unlikely that the authors were writing thoughts inconsistent with the prevailing ones in their communities. This is not to take away from their contributions as authors. The people who wrote these early pieces of literature have given us a wonderful voice from our early history. These early recordings of human thoughts are quite diverse, likely demonstrating the diversion that was already occurring between human groups and the developing civilizations.

The Universal God of Abraham

The universal God of Abraham was a significant step forward in human history, and represents left brain contribution to the concept of god. Up until that point, the god concept was driven by the sense of wonderment about the world coming from our vision-based cognition.

Thinking (left brain) about god can easily lead to the conclusion that there is only one God. Even today, it can be reasoned that, if there is a god, there can only be one God. It does not really make sense that there are different gods for different groups. There is only one observable world and each group is living within the same world. There can only be one God.

Abraham was born in Mesopotamia sometime around 2,000 BCE and his life is recorded in the Book of Genesis. He moved to Canaan, spent time in Egypt during a period of drought, and ended up moving back to the "promised land" in Canaan where his universal God promised to make him a great nation and to bless him and his followers.

Until Abraham each human grouping; whether town, city, or early civilization, had its own god (or gods) that served as the center of their group. Abraham introduced the concept that there really is only one God who is the god of everybody. The universal God of Abraham is the progenitor of the Jewish, Christian, and Islamic religions. All three religions share the original God of Abraham.

The first two commandments in the Judeo-Christian teaching are related to the fact that their God is universal:

- First commandment: "I am the Lord thy God. Thou shalt have no other gods before me."
- Second commandment: "Thou shalt not make unto thee any graven image, or any likeness of anything that is in heaven above, or that is in the earth beneath, or that is in the water under the earth: Thou shalt not bow down thyself to them, nor serve them."

The second commandment also clearly states that the universal God is invisible and not to be represented by any physical statues. This is a clear departure from previous gods and sets the stage for the same God to serve, or control, much larger areas. Individuals no longer need to have a dominating icon in their environment.

In our early development, groups were each led by their gods; therefore, gods also led them to war with one another. Human history is filled with wars fought along religious lines. Likewise, the universal God of Abraham also served as an aggressive war-like leader.

The Old Testament books are filled with human atrocities inflicted on one another. It is very clear that violence was a significant part of human life at those times. Because religion, or belief in a particular God, defined one group opposed to another, wars were fought between groups defined by their religion or God. This continues today.

CHAPTER 8

Civilizations and the Human Mind

Self and Group in Civilizations

Group-think and Human Advancement

Agriculture and animal domestication enabled us to go beyond being the dominant species on the planet. They were the means by which we began using the resources of our planet to be able to increase our numbers and to increase our comfort. Our human left-brain capabilities, especially the group left brain, had demonstrated their transcendent abilities.

Agriculture was only the first major collective effort of humans that resulted in tremendous acceleration of civilization development. We have had numerous similar explosive developments. Some are smaller than others, but each built upon the successes of previous technological development. Some of the other earlier technology explosions were invention of the wheel, invention of writing and an alphabet, and domestication of animals. Along the way there were other technology explosions such as the use of metals, the printing press, telescopes and microscopes, and the industrial revolution. More recent technology explosions include transportation (trains, cars, and planes), electricity, radio, television, etc. Each new development was a revolution that comprised a very fast pace of development because of the collective efforts of humans. The most recent technology explosion we've experienced is the computer age - leading to the age of information. The computer revolution produced the doubling phenomenon, dubbed "Moore's Law", stating that computer technological development doubles every 18 months.

Our "group-think" has enabled the explosion of advances throughout human history. When we work together, we seemingly have unlimited development – as evidenced by the wonders of our current civilization.

At the core of it all, these large technological revolutions each required that people cooperate and contribute to the whole. Very close to our own ego is the desire and need to focus our efforts on the collective whole. We each possess a sense of group-responsibility.

Fueled by the ambitions of our ego, we feel a need to contribute to the whole. Without this need, we would have been unable to build the civilization that we see around us. On average, each human contributes to the whole and the whole is advanced to at least some small extent by each person's efforts. Without this collective cooperation, as fueled by the inner need of each person to do so, we would still be hunter/gatherers.

Self vs. Group in Civilizations

Development of our left-brain concept of group, oriented towards success, has led to the organization and characteristics of our current Civilizations. A large part of human groups, and the distinguishing characteristics among Civilizations, concern how the interface between self and group is organized and managed. The Self/Group axis is the oldest and most basic (Figure 10). This comes to us from the depths of our right brain, although the left brain has now played a significant role in this axis. This axis affects group and individual human behavior more significantly than any other.

Our Civilizations have developed strategies for defining the Self/ Group roles in our groups. Some of the highest moral discussions involve the relationship between the self and the group (or others), such as: fairness, proper behavior, rights of the individual, responsibilities of the individual. This also applies to smaller human groups. Each country, state, city, and county has sets of rules that define the role of the individual. Even fraternities, associations, clubs, and teams have sets of rules that structure the accepted and expected behaviors. If a small group has no written set of rules, then there is an unwritten code of conduct accepted by members of the group.

The Self/Group differentiation is the most critical factor behind human behavior. It is critical for our behaviors as individuals and also collectively within our groups. It is also likely that the Self/Group axis is the most important axis for the Darwinian survival of our species.

Self and Group as Behavior Motivators

What is it that motivates or drives our ego in guiding our behavior?

Foremost, we are driven by our right brain survival needs. Survival includes bodily protection as well as food and warmth. However, we have other needs that are beyond basic survival such as needs for affection, sexual satisfaction, happiness, etc. We are also driven by our own left brain personal desires. Self-desires can include a new car, fine clothes, or a nice dining experience at a restaurant. Early human self-desires probably included skin paint, hand-made jewelry, and perhaps the warmest spot at the fire.

> *Most fundamentally we are driven by the needs of self and the desires of ego. Our right-brain needs are the most fundamental human motivators and probably also the strongest. However, since our right-brain self needs have largely been met in advanced civilizations, our left-brain desires have become the larger behavior motivators.*

However, the needs and desires of the group also motivate individual human behavior.

As we banded together in small groups, we could not behave solely as self-interested individuals. Each human derived benefit from being in the group, but in return each human had obligations and responsibilities to the group. Each human could not be solely motivated by self-desire, but also became motivated by the group needs. Coming from our right brain, we feel a need to contribute to the group. Our left-brain correlate of this is a definable obligation or responsibility to the group. This is usually in the form of rules and regulations.

The bond we feel with our group members is very strong and comes to us from our right-brain sense of "group". It comes from deep within the animal world. Many mammals bond in family units and derive benefits of protection and nurturing of the young. Many animals have herding instincts that cause them to bond together for protection. Some predators bond together for food acquisition. These types of bonding in animals provide benefits to each individual animal. Bees and ants appear to have an advanced type of bonding that transcends the bonding of most other animals. Each individual bee and ant makes specific contributions to the group with quite impressive organizational results. The behavior of each bee and ant appears motivated by the group needs.

Each individual is motivated, at some level, by meeting the group needs. This is an essential part of life. Life, as we see it expressed on this planet, is based upon the Darwinian survival and development of species. The behavior of each individual within a species is at least partly motivated by the needs of the group. Bonding together and meeting group needs is a fundamental part of life and the human mind. This is an essential part of life that we cannot really rationalize. It just is.

> *Although each person has clear self-interests that motivate their behavior, each person is also motivated by the needs of the group. Our motivation to meet the needs of the group comes from deep within us - from the depths of life that come to us from our right brain.*

We each feel a group-responsibility. In earlier days, it is likely that one human shared their hunting success with another, but in return the other made fire and cooked the meat. Group-responsibility also required consideration of the needs of others. For example, there was likely an understood dictum not to steal food from another group member, not to kill one another, and not to have forced sex with another, etc. These were the beginnings of morals, ethics and law. Today our level of cooperation with one another is much more complex. However, we continue to have many personal interactions with others that require our actions be guided by group-responsibility. At another level, our group interactions involve governmental institutions, exchange of materials and services for money, taxation, etc.

Our self-desires and our group-responsibility are fundamental motivators that drive our behavior. The advantages of meeting self-desires accrue directly to the individual. The advantages of meeting group-responsibility accrue to the group and secondarily to the individual through group success.

We are each motivated by both our self-desire and by our group-responsibility. Often they conflict with one another and we must choose which will guide our behavior. For example, our self-desire may cause us to simply take something we see in a store; our group-responsibility tells us this is considered stealing and we choose to restrain ourselves. Our self-desire tells us we would like to have a second piece of chocolate cake, but a sense of fairness that emanates from group-responsibility tells us to wait because others at the table have not yet had theirs.

Self-desire is almost certainly more fundamental to each person than group-responsibility, but both strongly influence our behavior.

Ultimately, group success is what is important to survival and evolution of Homo sapiens. Ultimately, group success is also what is most important for individual success because of the numerous benefits derived from well developed group dynamics, or civilization.

Role of Self-Desires in Civilization

Our most fundamental self-desires are bodily physical requirements that must be met such as food, water, body temperature maintenance, and protection from physical harm. These basic survival needs are essentially the same as the needs of animals. These are the most basic human motivators and are the Freudian Id. If we are deficient in any of these basic needs, we will be strongly driven to act to meet the deficiency.

Anyone who is reading this book is highly unlikely to have difficulty meeting the basic survival needs of self-desire. Unfortunately, however, there are many people in the world today who have difficulty meeting even basics such as food and shelter. This is a large problem, especially in the under-developed areas of the world, but also even in major developed countries such as the United States. For now, however, and not to belittle the problems of hunger in the world, this discussion will concentrate on the populations in developed countries for which basic survival is not a problem.

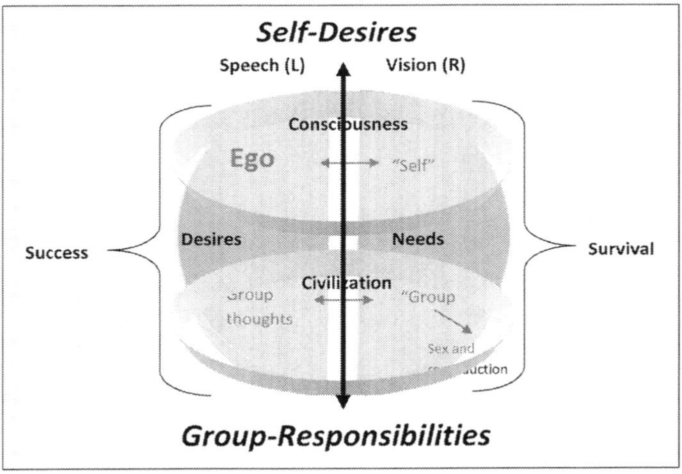

Figure 16. *The most fundamental axis that affects individual human behavior concerns our orientation towards satisfying self-desires vs. group-responsibilities. This axis is deeply embedded in the right brain; group-think in our groups and civilizations attempt to formally define it.*

When the base survival needs have been met, then the left brain self-desires of the Ego become strong behavior motivators. Humans each have personal desires that drive their behavior. We each desire things that elevate our own status. In many respects, materialism is representative of these desires. Although a base level of clothing is a "need" of the Id for warmth and protection, today we want a wardrobe of finer clothes in a mixture of style, function and color to enhance personal appearance and status. The corresponding desire in the early days of human development was probably to have the nicest animal pelt for a garment or the most attractive stone for a piece of jewelry. With the advent of agriculture and towns, this escalated to having the nicest dwelling and the best location. Today the availability of material things to satisfy our self-desires is almost limitless: cars, clothes, vacations, appliances, games, entertainment - just about anything money can buy.

Self-desires also go beyond physical items and extend to how we spend our time. When a person chooses to spend their morning watching TV instead of helping their neighbor lay sod, their behavior has been determined by self-desires. When we spend over-time at work to do a job and it is because we want the overtime pay and/or because it will help us towards a promotion, we are likewise motivated by self-desires. If we train athletically to keep our body in shape, it is also for our self-desires. If our behavior is motivated by self-esteem, self-importance, self-assuredness, self-respect, etc, it is motivated by self-desire. This is ego-centric behavior.

Everyone is motivated by self-desire. This is not necessarily bad. However, behaviors motivated by "self-desire" that are also perceived to conflict with group-responsibility are judged to be "selfish".

> *The rewards of behavior motivated by self-desires are clear. Such behaviors result in meeting personal needs. The rewards accrue to the individual. However, if all human behavior were purely driven by self-desires, then we would not have been successful as a species in building civilizations. In fact, any species in which behavior is motivated purely on the needs of the individual will not survive in a Darwinian world.*

There can be significant differences among human groups concerning self/group motivation. For example, a group of entrepreneurs will almost certainly be motivated more by self-desires than a non-profit group. The latter will be motivated more by the interests of the group. Likewise, and as developed earlier, there can be significant differences among civilizations. Individual behavior in Western Civilization is certainly motivated more by self-desires, and in Eastern Civilizations more by group-responsibility.

Role of Group-Responsibility in Civilization

Our left brain Ego separates us from nature and the animals around us; and it also often trumps the right brain sense of "self". As result, we feel (and *know*) that we occupy a special and elevated place in our world. We each perceive that there is something about us that is separate from nature. However, we each also know that every other human has an ego and also perceives their self as separate from nature. We feel an affinity with one another and a need for one another that causes us to bond together. In fact, the bond we feel with other humans is deeply ingrained in our very being. The strong bond that we humans feel for one another has enabled us to cooperate with one another and to develop civilizations.

The bond we feel with other humans is deeply ingrained in our very being and has enabled us to cooperate with one another and to develop civilizations.

The group is only as strong as the contributions of its members. Therefore, group development and strength is dependent upon the extent to which individuals contribute to the needs of the group. We cannot solely pursue our self-desires and still have a successful group. We must consider the group needs in our behavior.

If individuals on the whole do not meet the needs of the group, then the group will not be successful. A major part of our group-responsibility is to contribute to the welfare of the group. One way we do this is with the work that we perform. In the early days of human development this involved hunting, making shelter, providing child care, making jewelry, etc. When a person made a fire, s/he made it large enough for the group. When a person was good at making garments from animal hides, that person made them for others. Our current civilization is much more specialized, and individual contributions include those of earlier civilizations as well as such things as driving a bus, making baseball bats, accounting, software design, and the myriad other jobs that people in our civilization perform and that we as a group depend upon.

Our group-responsibility also requires that we be "civil" with others in the group. We must cooperate with others and treat them with respect. We should not lie, cheat, steal, or kill. It is our duty to not tread on the rights of others. This leads to ethics and morals. These group-responsibility principles are also collectively contained in something we call our "conscience".

Summary

Civilization would not be possible without the collective efforts of individuals. Our civilizations advance because, on the average, each person contributes to the advancement of our civilization. This is not to say that every person contributes to advancement. Hitler, Genghis Khan, and serial murderers cause more harm than good. But, there are more contributors than detractors. On average each human life makes civilization better. This individual contribution to the whole began in small groups of hunter-gatherers, has continued through the tremendous group size increases that began with agriculture, and has escalated to the cities, nations and the multi-nation civilizations of today. None of this would have happened without the sense of group-responsibility. The sense of group-responsibility is very close to the core of what it is to be human.

Early Right Brain Civilizations

The earliest human groups derived from the right-brain animal world from which we emerged. They were heavily based upon the herding and dominance hierarchy models that we observed in the animal world around us. Just as the gods of the earliest cities were large centralized icons, it appears that the socio-political organizations of the earliest cities were likewise organized as dominance hierarchies around god-like leaders.

Civilizations sprang from the early agricultural cities, in fact the word "civilization" is derived from the Latin word, civilis, meaning "city". These earliest civilizations, like the cities from which they grew, were organized around the right brain animal models that had been the previous norm for human group organization. These earliest (ancient) civilizations were organized similar to ant and bee colonies. Humans herded around the dominance hierarchy structure, which included a god concept at the center. Individual freedoms as we know them did not exist. The individual left brain ego was limited in terms of its ability to express itself or make contributions at the group level. As a group, our left brain group-think contributed mightily to our abilities to work together and harness the resources in our environment, but left-brain group think was not really contributing to our group management or leadership. We were organized in a dominance hierarchy with a god and/or queen bee figure at the pinnacle.

EGYPT

Certainly the Egyptian empire was one of the largest, most enduring, and most famous of the early civilizations. It began in about 3100 BCE and remained a separate culture and civilization until 332 BCE when conquered by Alexander the Great, with final Roman conquest in 30 BCE. The Egyptian Civilization endured for 3,000 years. The original Egyptian civilization no longer exists and today's Egypt is Islamic.

The Egyptian Civilization owed its strength, its rise to centralized power within the region, and its longevity to the Nile River. The Nile River's annual flood cycle provided lifeblood to the agriculture of the region and also made it well-circumscribed. The Egyptian empire benefited from being surrounded by un-crossable deserts on three sides; and therefore, only had to fend off intruders from the Isthmus of Suez.

One of Egypt's enduring characteristics was lack of change. Egypt was originally a collection of small farming cities whose cultures were unified by about 3,000 BCE. There was a collective benefit to joining together into the larger civilization. The larger collective group certainly had pooled resources that could not be attained by the individual cities. The larger collective group also discouraged, and probably ended, inter-city feuds and wars, and the large collective group also discouraged outsiders from tangling with it because of its size and resources. Evidence indicates that even during times of drought, when resources became scarce, the fabric of the society largely remained and people cooperated with one another. There is also evidence that robbing of earlier tombs when times became rough was orderly and sponsored by the state (Discovery Channel).

The hierarchical structure headed by the god-like Pharaoh kept this civilization rigidly organized and unchanging. The centralized state was extremely strong and individuals were tied to the state economically and religiously. The state provided security, a comfortable life (i.e., "success"), and religious beliefs. All evidence indicates that the people and workers received good care - even medical care. In return, Egyptian people were subservient (but not enslaved) to the state.

The Egyptian empire is famous for building its long-enduring pyramids, statues, and temples. These remain among the largest symbols on our planet, and most served to religiously unify the people of the Nile. The Egyptian empire was organized similarly to the dominance hierarchies of earlier cities. It was larger, so required larger symbols of the gods that served to cement the group into a functioning state. This basic organization is essentially the same as for the earliest of human groups (see Figure 14).

The Egyptian religion included a creation story and also showed obsession with a life after death. Even common Egyptians believed in an eternal soul, a last judgment, and resurrection after death. There was a very strong leader (King), who was mixed between human and God, that served as the center of the group. The hierarchy, or pecking order, in these civilizations was well-defined, with the largest mass of people living in complete subservience and without any hope or even thought of changing their lot. People seemed to just accept their position in life. They probably did not question their role for several reasons[2]. One was that it was totally outside

2 We see this yet today in the Hindu caste system. It is also the expected behavior in military units, or any group that is led by dictator. Adherence to group rules is the only behavior that is accepted or reinforced. This behavior is the same as the dominance hierarchy behavior that comes from, and which we still carry with us, from the animal world.

of their experience in life to do so. It was not their position to think or question the organization into which they were born, and their upbringing had not prepared them to do so. Our minds had not yet developed to that point. Concepts such as freedom and democracy had not yet been established. Even if they had capacity to question the way that life was set up, they would have had no ability to change it. Their life depended upon the civilization into which they were born and the rules of that life were guided from the top. The top provided everything to guide their life - including god and religion.

The Egyptian system provided success for the group insofar as the human mind had developed to that point. The system survived for 3,000 years - a record for civilization longevity. It was a rigid system and did not encourage or allow for advanced development of the human mind - certainly not for those at the bottom of the structure and possibly also not for those at the top. The rigidity of the system did not allow individual advanced thinking to emerge.

The Egyptian governance system may be viewed as the pinnacle development of the dominance hierarchy in human governance. The right-brain sense of "group" dominated the left-brain group-think in governance. The left-brain group think was evident in terms of the many accomplishments of Egyptians (especially the building programs), but it was subservient to the vision-based sense of group coming from the animal world in terms of group governance.

Theocracy in other Right Brain Civilizations

The strong god-based group structure with subservient classes of people observed in Egypt appears in other ancient civilizations, and also continues to some current civilizations. The ancient Egyptian form of government is now referred to as a "theocracy". The word was first coined by Joseph Flavius in the first century AD to refer to the god-centered organization of the Jews and is derived from the Greek word meaning "rule of god".

A theocracy is a form of government in which it is understood by the ruled that they are governed by a god or by individuals who are part god or at least divinely inspired. God is recognized as the head of the government.

> *This form of government, such as shown in the Egyptian model above, is possibly the oldest form of government and harkens back to the original small human groups. It is a dominance hierarchy model that places god at the head of the hierarchy.*

Scarpari (2006) reviews the characteristics of the earliest known Chinese Ancient Civilizations. He writes: "Social organization was generally based on a system of kinship that guaranteed the most powerful families the loyalty of immense clans." He also wrote: "The complexity of the wealthiest burials and finds of animal bones used for divination demonstrate the existence of social hierarchies and a dominant class that held religious authority."

The early Mesopotamian Civilizations had Ziggarat temples at the centers of their city-states. Priests would represent the gods and control the economy. The Incan empire was also a theocracy. The Inca king was considered the descendant of Inti, the sun God. Likewise, the Mayan Civilization was a theocracy, with each city-state ruled by royalty. Some Islamic states today have accepted Islam as their political foundation, effectively making them theocracies.

The Sudden Meeting of Old and New Civilizations

The ancient and theocratic civilizations in the Old World (i.e., Europe, Asia and Africa) could not survive the developing Western Civilization led first by the Greeks and then by the Romans. However, ancient civilizations in the New World (i.e., the American continents) such as the Aztec, Incan, and Mayan, because of their remoteness and complete lack of communication with the Old World were able to persist without outside influence until the discovery of the New World in 1492.

These New World ancient civilizations bore similarities to the Old World ancient civilizations. These theocratic civilizations were totalitarian ones built around totalitarian rulers who were associated with god. They were hierarchical societies headed by noble classes of warriors. The first Europeans to view these civilizations noted the cruelty of the rulers towards the masses of workers and towards other peoples. These societies also relied upon large working classes that appeared to have unquestioning support for the God-rulers. These unquestioning workers, kept in line by fear, were able to build large temples that rival the Egyptian pyramids in terms of size and magnificence. Of course, these temples and pyramids were part of the religion that played a major role in the society. The rulers were intimately involved with the control of that religion and used human sacrifice in those temples, often on a large scale, as part of their control tactics. In the dedication of the great pyramid of Tenochtitlan in 1489 as many as 20,000 people were sacrificed.

These ancient New World civilizations, like those of the Old World, were not based upon the free will of individuals. They also seem to bear resemblance to bee and ant colonies; individuals did not have self-determination and the hierarchical society maintained strict control by the ruler.

The clash of these ancient civilizations with the more advanced Western Civilization is very instructive. Atahualpa was the absolute monarch of the Incan nation and worshipped as a sun god. The Incans were the largest and most advanced civilization in the New World. Yet, in 1532 AD, the Spanish conquistador Francisco Pizarro, with 168 Spanish soldiers was able to easily take over the Incan empire of 12 million people and its army of 80,000 soldiers. How was this possible?

In this most remarkable clash of Western Civilization with an ancient civilization, Pizarro was able to quickly subdue the Incan nation. Jared Diamond provides first-hand accounts from some of the Spanish soldiers. First of all, the soldiers were so scared by the massive display of the Incan military manpower and the extravagant and opulent display of power wielded by Atahualpa that many "urinated without noticing it, out of sheer terror." However, Pizarro outsmarted the Incans by tricking them into thinking they came in peace. Pizarro and his men were probably much more skilled at deception than the Incans had ever previously experienced. Pizarro and his men also set a fairly transparent trap into which Atahualpa, in all his glory and with his several layers of high chiefs and councilors, unsuspectingly and ceremoniously was carried. They out-thought the

Incans – unfortunately deceit is one of the attributes of advanced human thinking. The Spaniards also had a large advantage in terms of having 62 horses (horses were not available in the New World) and steel weapons. Pizarro's dozen muskets were probably more psychological than tactical. The superiority of weapons by itself cannot explain overcoming the almost 500:1 manpower superiority of the Incan military.

A key to the Incan conquest was the capture of Atahualpa and the effects it had upon the entire Incan Civilization. When the God-ruler was plucked from the civilization, the entire society folded - just like plucking the queen bee. It is likely that neither the group-think nor the thinking of individuals nor the breadth of experience of the Incans was any match for the thinking abilities that Western Civilization had given to Pizarro and his men. The Incans were no match for the superiority of the Western Civilization mind's cunning.

Also, the Pizzaro "conquest" of the Peruvian Incans can give us further insight into an old Theocracy.

> *In Cuzco in 1589, Don Mancio Serra de Leguisamo - one of the last survivors of the original conquerors of Peru—wrote in the preamble of his will, the following, in parts:*
>
> *"We found these kingdoms in such good order, and then said Incas governed them in such wise [manner] that throughout them there was not a thief, nor a vicious man, nor an adulteress, nor was a bad woman admitted among them, nor were there immoral people. The men had honest and useful occupations. The lands, forests, mines, pastures, houses and all kinds of products were regulated and distributed in such sort that each one knew his property without any other person seizing it or occupying it, nor were there law suits respecting it… the motive which obliges me to make this statement is the discharge of my conscience, as I find myself guilty. For we have destroyed by our evil example, the people who had such a government as was enjoyed by these natives. They were so free from the committal of crimes or excesses, as well men as women, that the Indian who had 100,000 pesos worth of gold or silver in his house, left it open merely placing a small stick against the door, as a sign*

that its master was out. With that, according to their custom, no one could enter or take anything that was there. When they saw that we put locks and keys on our doors, they supposed that it was from fear of them, that they might not kill us, but not because they believed that anyone would steal the property of another. So that when they found that we had thieves among us, and men who sought to make their daughters commit sin, they despised us." Attributed to Cobo

The above description of the Incan behavior provides insight to a very moral and well-behaved society - even though it was also very capable of cruelty. This tranquility seems similar to that found in the Egyptian Civilization. God is in charge! When god is in charge, everybody behaves. The god-mandated behavior is the only way to successfully survive in such a culture. The behavior patterns are rigidly laid out and so strongly held by the group that enforcement is perhaps not even necessary.

THEOCRACY – AN ANIMAL MODEL?

It is tempting to compare the organization of the Egyptian and other ancient civilizations to something we see in the animal kingdom today – ant and bee colonies. Such animal colonies are highly organized with a queen at the top and various levels of subservient individuals below the queen. There are several classes of workers, each with distinct roles in the colony or community. This organization resembles ancient human civilizations.

J.M. Roberts, author of A Short History of the World, writes: "Most animals which live in groups - ants, bees, herds of deer - look very well-regulated. It seems that they are better at keeping rules in their societies than human beings. Yet that is only because they are in fact very different from humans. They are not actually obeying rules (as we understand them) at all, but are behaving almost automatically; they do things because they are programmed by their genes or by patterns of behavior imprinted so deep that we call them "instincts". They could not behave otherwise if they wanted to, indeed, they cannot want to."

These animal models of group behavior, which served as the models for the earliest human civilizations, are those developed with vision-based minds coming from the animal world. There were no thoughts.

J.M Roberts further states that: "Human history began when the inheritance of genetics and behavior which had until then provided the only means of survival was first broken through by *conscious choice*" (italics added). This statement is consistent with the story of Adam and Eve in which Adam's choice was the first step in our separation from Nature.

Animals seem to make choices such as when to eat, sleep, or hunt - but since they do not have words, their consciousness and means of making a choice must be different than ours. They certainly don't debate with themselves about what to do. Only humans have a thinking consciousness and can make thinking decisions. Animals and our pre-human ancestors did not have a thinking consciousness and reacted more by instinct and automatic reflex.

> *The group-think of Homo sapiens in the earliest civilizations was not as sophisticated as today. The earliest civilizations had evolved from the vision-based animal world.*

Just as worker bees and ants seem to work incessantly to build their colonies, the Egyptian workers were able to build monumental structures like the pyramids that remain for us to see yet today. Their group-thinking was likely more like ants and bees than our current group-thinking.

Today we take freedom of thought and expression to be fundamental to what it is to be human. This is a characteristic of Western Civilization. Such individualism was probably unheard of and un-thought of in these early civilizations. The state of human thought was elementary compared to today. Even the earliest writings, as discussed earlier, show attribution of actions and speaking to individual gods. The early civilizations were probably the developmental endpoint of the groups that first formed around campfires, evolved into agricultural groups, and then into clusters of cities. The ruler at the top had absolute authority and was also inseparable from the god and religion of the civilization.

Living in a theocracy seems very limiting to us, because we are so used to having personal freedom. However, at that time, subservience probably met our mind capabilities and, in balance, the benefits we received from it outweighed any other options.

However, was life really uncomfortable or poor in quality for the people? The Incans seemed to live very comfortable lives. There is no record of any rebellions or bad behavior among Egyptians for their 3,000 years of rule. We haven't come close to that record; in fact, the 2,000 years since then have largely been filled with hatred and war.

The human mind was growing. These older civilizations were great at satisfying and harnessing both the right and left-brain groups, but were very rigid and did not allow growth of the sense of self and, especially, the left-brain ego. The left-brain group-think was being harnessed, as demonstrated by agriculture, animal domestication, and other advances in harnessing nature for our benefit. These early groupings were based upon unquestioned deference and belief in a God, and unquestioned obedience to the God-run state. However, our thinking ability was not yet applied to the leadership or structure of our groups. There also was little room for individual ego expression. There was no room for ego to question things. The second round of civilizations allowed for individual participation and human thinking became part of group governance.

The Axis Age

The German philosopher Karl Jaspers is credited with first defining the Axis Age. He used the term to describe the period roughly from 800 BCE to 200 BCE, during which human thinking appeared throughout much of the Old World. Individual great thinkers had extremely large influence on civilizations and their structures.

The Axis Age launched the next round of civilizations - the same civilizations in which we presently live. The primary shift that occurred was the greater participation of the left brain, both on a group and individual level, in human governance. At about this time, hugely influential thinkers influenced large groups of people with their messages. The written word was powerful in influencing large groups of people. The messages of these thought leaders led to the development of the next stage of Civilizations.

The Civilizations could now be structured around a system of unique thoughts or beliefs. This enabled larger groups of people to be managed within a group. The system of thoughts or beliefs served as a strong center for the group.

GIANTS OF THE AXIS AGE

Although there were many great thought leaders at about this time, those who have had the greatest and longest lasting influences on current civilizations are:

- Siddh□ rtha Gautama, or Buddha, of India, approximately 563 BCE to 483 BCE
- Confucius, China, 551 BCE – 479 BCE
- Socrates, Greece, 469 BC–399 BC

We still see their influence, very strongly, in today's world. In fact, the seeds of most of today's major civilizations can be found dating back to this period. These were the men who broke out from under the stifling belief and obedience systems existent up until then. The left-brain ego was now expressing itself over large populations of people in the world. The individual mind was now competing for the group organization and leadership. Blind obedience to the right-brain visual world, and its systems, was being questioned. There was now an emerging and developing left-brain guidance and think ability. The left-brain group began gaining dominance, but it needed individual human leaders to get them past the group right.

The breakthroughs attributed to Buddha, Confucius, and Socrates were immense in our history. However, they were also reporters from their eras and they were writing about their times. The left brain of humans was probably developing nicely across the population. The left brain had shown its prowess by that time. Thinking humans and their group left brain skills had demonstrated their ability to allay the right brain (the "seed of life") concern about survival. And, everyone enjoyed the success they were experiencing. At that time, it certainly felt "successful" to be living with nice clothes, within walls that separated us from nature, and with some other nice things such as art, music, and other amenities. I think we can now begin to use the word "people" to refer to those living at that time.

> *Homo sapiens have not since had a group of thought leaders who have had such influence over the entire species. They allowed the left brain of man (success-driven) to get out from under domination by the right brain (survival-driven). Our species has not had such a revolution since.*

The thought leaders of the Axis Age established left-brain input as a partner with our right brain in guiding our human destiny - both on the group and the self levels. Prior to that time, the right brain was largely in control at our species command level. These thought leaders essentially established the rules by which the balance between right and left brains interacted at the group, or civilization level. The rules they established can be seen today in the differences between current major civilizations.

Buddha, Confucius, and Socrates created the opportunities for the individual left brain (ego) to be expressed more fully. The ego was now recognized and heard at the species command level. Individualism had emerged as an element in the behavior of our species. We could say that it became programmed into us through the common neural circuitry that we are able to develop (Ramachandran).

Giants of the Axis Age and Current Civilizations

The teachings of each of these three giants (Buddha, Confucius, and Socrates) had significant and different effects upon how the left brain and right-brain senses of group interacted in the guidance of the group. Their different theories on truths about life served as the foundations for different civilizations and cultures. These differences are still existent and very apparent in civilization differences today. In fact, their ideas have blossomed and are more influential today than during their lives.

BUDDHA, INDIA, APPROXIMATELY 563 BCE TO 483 BCE

The history of India goes back to the Harappan Civilization (2500-1500 BCE) which was located in the Indus River Valley in current day Pakistan and NW India. Much is yet to be known about the Harappan Civilization, but it appears to have been well-developed by the standards of the day. Their written language has not yet been de-coded. It appears that the Aryans, a people not yet well-identified, settled the Harappan Civilization from the north. The Harappan Civilization failed, likely because of climate change affecting the monsoons and/or depletion of forest resources. From there, humans settled in the Ganges River Valley in the north of current-day India.

The origins of the caste system are not known, but it appears to go back to the Harappan era. The caste system is a rigid system in which a person's role in life is defined by the caste into which they are born. Although this system is now forbidden by current governments, remnants still remain in India today. The caste system is a vestige of a right-brain dominance hierarchy system.

Many thinkers emerged from the Ganges area. The most famous and influential was Siddhartha Gautama (563 BCE to 483 BCE) - who came to be known as "Buddha" which means "awakened one", or "the enlightened one." He attained enlightenment sitting under a pipal (fig) tree, now revered as the Bodhi tree in the Gaya District of India. He came from a princely caste but then set out on a road trip seeking truth and enlightenment. He and five disciples wandered the Ganges plain preaching for 40 years. His last words were: "All created things must pass. Strive on diligently." Buddha's teachings remained local for 200 years.

BUDDHIST TEACHINGS

Buddhism has become a complex life-guidance system with several nuances, sects, and even disagreement among Buddhist leaders. Below I attempt to summarize the essential aspects of Buddhism.

First of all, Buddhism does not teach a god, in fact it is atheistic. Buddhism is based upon pure morality and universal values. Buddhism is also very introspective and teaches that we can find truth about life through such introspection. Hence, meditation is a part of Buddhism.

A central part of Buddhist teaching is the four Noble Truths:

1. Life means suffering. Because we and the world in which we live are imperfect, we necessarily endure suffering in life. Life can also contain happy events, but in the end, life is imperfect and impermanent. Suffering and death are inevitable parts of life.
2. The origin of suffering is attachment. Suffering comes to us because of our attachments to things in life. We have attachments to physical objects, ideas, and to the "self". Our attachments come in such forms as passion, lust, desire, pursuit of fame and wealth, craving, and clinging. All things in life, including the "self", are transient in nature; therefore, attachments necessarily lead to suffering. Belief in god is simply one of the attachments.
3. The cessation of suffering is attainable. Suffering can be overcome by removing its causes. We can eliminate suffering if we can unmake, or lose our cravings and conceptual attachments. We need to become dispassionate about all attachments, and then can end our suffering and attain the state of Nirvana. Nirvana is freedom from worries, troubles, complexes, fabrications and ideas.
4. The path to the cessation of suffering. Buddha describes the Eightfold path to end suffering. The path is the middle way between self-indulgence (hedonism) and self-mortification (self-punishment).

We typically have rebirth into several subsequent lifetimes. This rebirth can build upon the strides we have made in previous lives along the path leading to the end of suffering.

The "self" is actually an illusion. Each of us is simply a part of life that is the Universe. In this way all living things are connected. Buddhism teaches respect for all living things. This is why animals are treated so respectfully in Buddhist countries and vegetarianism is common.

In effect, Buddhism is based upon the following principles:

- The four noble truths and the path to end suffering
- Respect for all living things
- Compassion for others and non-violence
- Seek truth through behavior and introspection
- Life is universal
- The self is illusory and just part of life

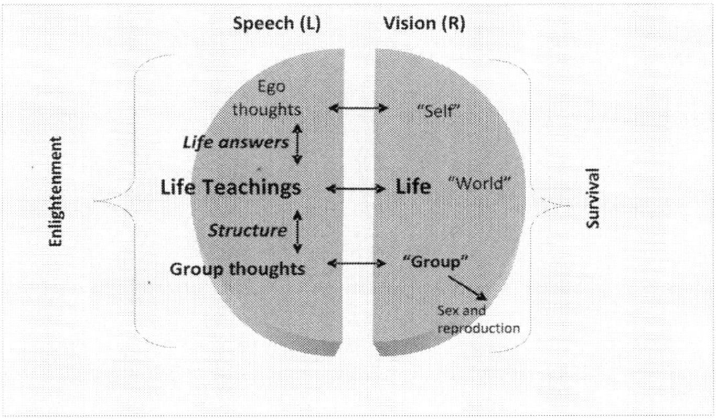

Figure 17. *The Buddhist sensory mind. Universal Life, coming from the right side, is central to the Buddhist world. The rules of life, or the Buddhist life teachings, structure the individual thoughts and relationships with the group. The "self" is considered illusory, and because of respect, compassion and non-violence towards others and all living things,* **group** *is emphasized over ego and self. Success is defined as attaining enlightenment, or Nirvana. Nirvana is difficult to explain because it codifies a right-brain concept.*

The Buddhist sensory mind, shown in the Figure is very different than the previous god and right-brain based models. God is replaced by a universal life that is in all living things. The Buddhist life teachings de-emphasize the ego and self, and instead favor good relationships with the group and other living things. Perhaps most importantly, success is defined in spiritual terms (enlightenment) and not in earthly pleasures. Buddhism and its subsequent influences on countries such as India has always been pacifist.

Buddhism Influences

Emperor Ashoka the Great (273–232 BCE) unified the Indian subcontinent as the Mauryan Empire. He was so appalled by the personal horrors of one of his bloody conquests that he converted to Buddhism. Thereafter, he renounced violence and promoted Buddhism by building stupas (Buddhist religious monuments) and enjoining all those in the empire to follow the Buddhist ways including respect for all living things.

Ashoka the Great also sent emissaries to various countries, even as far west as Greece, spreading the wisdom of Buddhism. Ashoka's acceptance and propagation of Buddhism is largely responsible for its widespread acceptance and influence in India and elsewhere, perhaps even more influential than Emperor Constantine's affect on the spread of Christianity.

Hinduism is the religion of South Asia, and perhaps more specifically, of India. Hinduism is not the same as Buddhism, but Buddhist teachings are strongly incorporated into Hinduism. The roots of Hinduism pre-date Buddha and are contained in very old writings such as the Vedas and the Mahabharata. Neither authors nor time of origins of either document are well known. The Mahabharata is an epic tale of a war that scholars have not yet been able to identify. It is fair to say that the teachings in these documents and their events served as a back drop for the teachings of Buddha.

The effects of Buddhism were strongly displayed through the leadership of Mahatma Gandhi leading to the end of British occupation of India in 1948. The Indians were effectively able to end British rule through non-violence and simply standing up for what was right. The Indians lost some battles in which they simply stood up and didn't fight, but they won the overall "war".

Confucius, China, 551 BCE – 479 BCE

China was the last of the great Civilizations to develop independently in the Old World. The Chinese civilizations developed 1,000 years after the Mesopotamian Civilizations, or about 2,000 BCE. By tradition, and probably pre-dating Confucius, the Chinese have great respect for their lineage and the wisdom of their ancestors.

Confucius strongly believed in the good in life and taught that individuals and states should be moral. The teachings of Confucius are largely contained in five ancient Chinese books which have served to guide Chinese society, government, literature, and religion. One of these books, the I Ching, is famously recognized as a Chinese book of wisdom. Confucianism became the state ideology in 136 BC and remained in that role until the early 20th century.

Confucian philosophy emphasizes personal and governmental morality, correctness of social relationships, justice and sincerity. Ritual and reverence for ancestors are large parts in maintaining moral order. These values serve as a foundation for Chinese culture.

Confucianism, like Buddhism, is not based upon a god. Instead, it is based upon sets of moral principles attributed to "Tao". Tao is the harmonious system of earth, nature and the cosmos. Tao is a right brain concept and difficult to describe. It is rather like a doctrine or principle representing the fundamental harmony and natural order of the universe. Tao is the source of harmony in nature, and refers to ideal morals and ethics.

Confucius teaches that everyone should be taught what is good. If people are taught what is good, then they will act accordingly, enforcement will not be required, and it will result in a society that is harmonious with nature. It is especially important to teach good to rulers. Everyone needs to be taught good from bad; this results in the ideal government.

Chinese rulers were said to have the Mandate of Heaven. This is a traditional concept similar to the European Divine Right of Kings, but different in a major way. The Divine Right of Kings is blessed by god. The Mandate of Heaven depends upon the talents and conduct of the particular ruler at being moral and virtuous. The Mandate of Heaven is not obtained by birth and the mandate can be withdrawn (by the ruled) for rulers who are not good. The Mandate would transfer to the person who would be good.

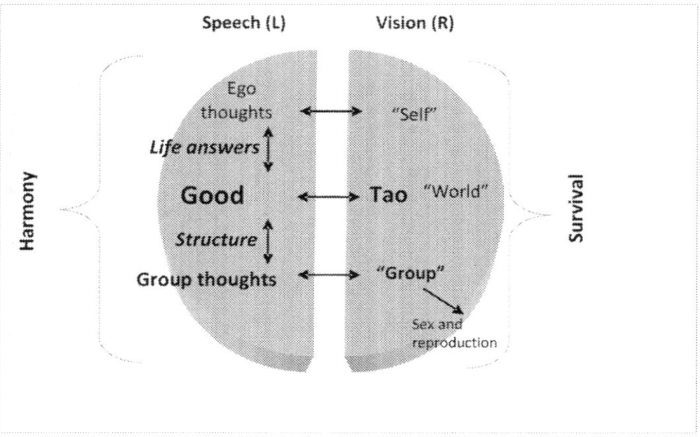

Figure 18. *The Confucius sensory mind. Tao, or life truth and harmony, comes from the right side and represents the ideal. The goal is to teach "good" to people and rulers in order to create a harmonious society. Confucius emphasized that the needs and good of the* ***group*** *were more important than those of the individual.*

Until 200 AD, China was totally isolated; they did not interact with or need anything from the outside world. With the opening of the Silk Road, trade and contact with India and points east developed. India was the primary part of the world that was opened to China at that time. China was already very spiritual, as encapsulated in the teachings of Confucius. The main thing that China wanted and took from India was the spiritual teachings of the Buddha, which have been at least partly included in current Chinese culture and religion.

The Chinese have never developed the concept of a god. The Western idea of a personal god does not exist in China. However, the rituals and morality belief system of Buddhism were easily accepted in China because of their compatibility.

The teachings of Buddha and Confucius both acknowledge an ultimate truth in life towards which individuals and groups should aspire. They were both thought leaders who were able to influence large populations of people with their rational thoughts. The civilizations that spawned from their teachings were no longer based upon pure dominance hierarchies.

Socrates, Greece, 469 BC–399 BC

The roots of current Western Civilization are found in ancient Greece. Although there were many great contributors from the Greek classical era, most would acknowledge the primary thought leader was Socrates. He was an Athenian philosopher who is known for the "Socratic method" of continued questioning and not taking a point of view until the person being questioned arrives at the answer. Socrates is acknowledged as a great teacher, but did not directly leave us any writings. He is famous mostly through the writings of his student Plato (427 BC -347 BC) and Plato's student Aristotle (384-322 BC).

> *These Greek philosophers were the first to explore and define human deductive reasoning and logic. They also made significant contributions to development of the scientific method. In effect, they were the thought leaders who examined the left-brain thinking capabilities and placed them in a leadership role.*

The Greeks developed an intellect and intellectual methods that still astound today. During a period of only about 400 years they engaged in a left-brain inquiry into life and nature. Many of the issues with which they dealt may seem trivial to us today. However, at that time they were just being discovered. For example, Thales came to the conclusion that the world could be understood by human investigation and that we did not need to rely on gods to explain everything - a major step forward. Thales also proposed that observable objects in the world can be reduced to more fundamental components, such as water and earth. Democritus actually proposed the concept that the world is built from a finite set of building blocks such as atoms. However, like many Greek discoveries and ideas, they lay fallow until the Renaissance almost 2,000 years later. The Greeks also developed arithmetic and geometry, even identifying some of the unique relationships such as between the diameter of a circle and its circumference (ϖ) and the Pythagorean equation that relates the square of the hypotenuse in a right triangle to the sum of the squares of its other two sides. Hippocrates began the scientific study of the body and health and is considered the father of medicine. Herodotus is considered the first historian. This brief list does not even begin to cover all of the academic areas developed by the Greeks. All of these contributions clearly emanate from greater emergence of left brain thinking.

The works from Socrates and his students are still considered to be seminal contributions in philosophy and other sciences. They investigated perception, moral truths, human reason, logic, politics, human inter-relations, division of the sciences into specialties, among many others.

It is no wonder, that even today, the Greek philosophers continue to be studied. This was the first true coming of the left brain as a centerpiece in leading the affairs of humans. The Greeks were uncovering totally new territory in our mind. They were able to explore this virgin territory unencumbered by subsequent discoveries and evolutionary mind development. They were certainly closer to the core of operation of the left brain than anyone today could possibly be. Since they were discovering new ground, they were able to describe and analyze human reasoning and thought in a manner never since possible. Greek philosophy is still a standard bearer today.

The Greeks did not have a clearly defined religious doctrine. There was no enforced religion. Instead, they had a pantheon of gods, each of whom was a specialist in certain areas. For example: Poseidon, was god of the seas, Hermes, god of merchants, Ares, god of war, Hades, god of the underworld, Aphrodite, goddess of love and beauty, etc. In addition, there were numerous mythical heroes and heroines such as Atlas, Phoebe, and Eros who interplayed with the gods. The Greek religion consisted of mythology about their gods and other fictitious characters.

> *The Greek mind was primarily concerned with human reasoning and abilities. The main function of the Greek mythological tales seemed to be to account for those things they could not reason.*

Reason, logic, and deduction are distinctly human characteristics associated with our ego. They are part of the verbal thought process of the left brain. Reasoning emphasizes one's own sense of ego. Reasoning emphasizes the sense of individualism and ultimately is intricately tied to democracy. Reasoning leads to individualism. This sense of individualism did not exist in the ancient civilizations that were organized primarily around non-verbal right-brain beliefs and instincts about the world.

> *Development of reasoning and logic also leads directly to a greater sense of individualism, because reasoning and logic are distinctly associated with mental activity experienced by the ego. This larger sense of individualism directly leads to democracy - which the Greeks famously implemented.*

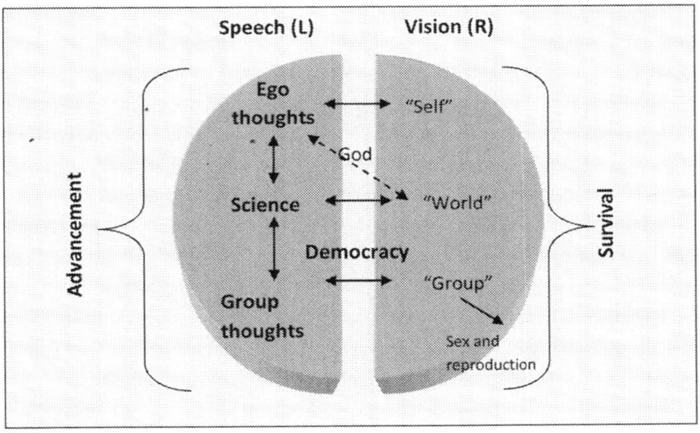

Figure 19. *The Greeks emphasized the* **left brain** *in both individuals and also in group leadership with the introduction of reasoning. The method of organizing the group was democracy, which enables individuals to vote with both their left-brain thinking and their right-brain feelings.* **Science** *became the method used to define the truth about the world. Individual human reasoning and group thoughts interacted with and were guided by science. They had a pantheon of gods who were more mythological than fundamental. The goal was advancement of the individual and society.*

Impact of the Greek Miracle

The Greeks totally shook up human development and civilization by exploring and codifying the cognitive abilities of the left brain. The left brain flexed its muscles and wrested major control of human destiny from the right brain. Human thought took control from instinct.

By introducing reason and thought, the Greeks distributed the knowing to everyone. Each person's individualism was established and recognized. Each person could think about his/her own ego and recognize its thinking capabilities as being part of their ego. Communication mechanisms enabled the thoughts of individuals to be aired at the group level and, if accepted, could be implemented by the group. This was not possible in earlier civilizations.

Certainly, at some point along our evolutionary development, humans did not have sufficient left-brain deductive reasoning to guide our behavior. There must have been some point along our evolutionary path where, in a large percentage of humans, reasoning had developed to the extent that we would allow it to guide us. Such development was probably occurring in the ancient civilizations, but the rigid and inflexible hierarchy of the civilization suppressed expression of such individualism. The relatively small and isolated cities of Greece were ideal environments, at the right evolutionary time, for this revolution to occur.

Individualism became more easily expressed during the time of the Greeks. This came from the left brain. However, we were still emerging from controls established by the survival instincts of right brain. The instincts of the right brain did not go away - they were still there and just as strong as ever. These instincts included our needs and responsibilities to the group. Even though we had learned the individualism of the left brain, we continued to experience the feelings and instincts of the right brain.

Equally important with the introduction of reason, the Greeks also introduced democracy.

Democracy was an extremely important part of the Greek group think and was the main form of group governance. Democracy enables individuals to each contribute (vote) to the group governance. Do people vote with their left-brain logic or their right-brain feelings? Obviously, it depends upon the individual and the issue being voted upon, but the global answer is that people vote with some combination of right and left brain inputs. Democracy engages and includes both the right brain and the left brain in group governance.

Democracy enables each person to contribute (vote) to the group using whatever combination of left-brain reasoning and right-brain intuition they desire. Democracy is a clever group governance system that enables both the right and left brains to participate.

The Greek and the ensuing Roman Civilizations were fueled mostly by application of the left-brain abilities at both the individual and group levels. One of the keys was the relative ease with which individuals could contribute ideas to be incorporated into the group. Individuals with good ideas could have an affect at the group level. Reason, logic, and the scientific method enabled tremendous advancements in the human ability to use and control the world around us. Of course, right brain functioning still existed in the Greek and Roman eras, but it was the new development of the left brain that fueled their growth and accomplishments.

The Greek philosophers clearly established our speech-based brain as the only way in which we could have true knowledge of reality, and demoted the vision-based brain as illusory and not a trusted view of reality. The Greek philosophers and other Greek minds established the left brain as being in control of Western Civilization, an operational mode that continues in Western Civilization yet today. Western Civilization has had amazing accomplishments as result.

THE AXIS AGE IN PERSPECTIVE

"Survival" will always trump "success" as a motivator when individual or species survival is called into question. Therefore, our species command comes to us through the right-brain sense of group. Although species command comes to our mind through the vision-based right brain, it goes deeper than that. Life began on this planet about four billion years ago, and the building blocks for life appear to have come from space via meteorites (amino acids discovered on meteorites, Birth of the Earth, History Channel). Our vision-based cognition only goes back about 570 million years ago.

The history of *Homo sapiens* on this planet has been the story of the emergence of our speech-based left-brain cognition. The major left-brain steps up to the Axis Age are:

1. Speaking enables our separation from animals and conquering the earth.
2. Our left-brain abilities enable us to harness nature for our own use with agriculture and animal domestication.
3. Our early groups and ancient civilizations come from the vision-based world of nature.
4. The Universal God of Abraham is an application of the left brain to the concept of god.
5. In the Axis Age the left brain steps up to play a role in human governance along with the right-brain sense of group. This is accompanied by, and enabled by, emergence of the individual (ego) at large group levels.

Western Civilization History – Left Brain, then Right, then Left again

The major events in Western Civilization history demonstrate the evolutionary struggles and relationships between the left and right brains in governing our species.

Western Civilization began when, for the first time in Life on this planet, the Greeks and then the Romans, included the left brain into formal group governance. Western Civilization lost left brain governance, for reasons discussed below, and right brain governance prevailed during the Dark Ages. The left brain began it's re-emergence into formal group affairs and governance during the Renaissance and has continued to today.

Here is the interpreted history of Western Civilization:

The Greeks established the left brain as the primary controller of Western Civilization. The Romans embraced the Greek mind and used the left brain to develop Western Civilization to sophistication and accomplishments never before attained. However, when left brain control of Western Civilization shifted from group-think (democracy in the Roman Republic) to control by individual ego (Emperors and the Roman Empire), the seeds for demise of Western Civilization had been sown. Right brain leadership replaced left brain Roman rule when Rome crumbled. The right brain ruled during the Dark Ages; the left brain re-emerged at the time of the Renaissance.

The Greeks

The Greek Civilization (roughly 750 BCE to 350 BCE) was comprised of a relatively loosely knit group of cities on the Greek peninsula. The Greek Peninsula has deep inlets and highlands that afford fairly protected locations for cities, the inland areas provided good farming. The Greeks were good at navigating the seas, and spread their ideas mainly through colonization over sea routes. They colonized large areas of Sicily, Italy, the northern African coast, the northern Aegean coast, and all around the Black Sea.

The Iliad and the *Odyssey* by Homer are among the oldest known literary writings from antiquity. Little is known about Homer, although the poems were probably written around 700 BCE and were likely stories that had been verbally recited for many years before they were committed to paper. Odysseus, the main character, was a cultural hero among the early Greeks and the poems were a staple of Greek education. Odysseus was probably the first Western hero. He was a wanderer and adventurer who gloried in his quest for life ventures. In many ways he epitomized the Greek quest for knowledge.

The Greeks were the first peoples to implement democratic forms of government. They were the first to introduce the concept of a citizen with rights in government. Each city had a different form of such government: ranging from oligarchy in which a city was ruled by aristocracy to true democracy run by votes and representation of all men. Sparta and

Athens are classical examples of the latter and former respectively. Many Greek cities used Athens as a government model; however, many other Greek cities preferred their oligarchic rule (especially the ruling aristocrats) and this caused divisiveness among the Greeks that lead to internal war (Peloponnesian War).

The great age of classical Greece ended with conquest by the Macedonian armies under Philip and Alexander the Great in 335 BCE. However, the Macedonians considered themselves Greek and through their numerous other conquests helped to spread widely the Greek language, ideas and culture.

The Romans

The Romans accepted and applied the operating knowledge of the left brain that was discovered and described by the Greeks. Their main contribution was in applying such knowledge to the world around them. They built a civilization that dominated the Western world for 1,000 years. Our current Western Civilization has developed directly from the Greek and Roman contributions.

The city of Rome had its origins around 750 BCE. Rome gained its independence from Etruscan rule and established a Greek-inspired republic around 510 BCE, which date is usually considered the beginning of the Roman Republic. The Roman Republic grew slowly during the next couple of centuries under the strong influence of the Greeks and their culture. The Carthaginians were the last remaining large rival of the Romans, and they were defeated by 202 BCE. The three centuries from about 150 BCE to 150 CE were the high point of the Roman Republic and Empire. During these years the Roman Empire encompassed nearly all of Europe, northern Africa, and Western Asia. Western Civilization reached a peak during these years that was not attained again for about 1,500 years - during the Renaissance.

The Romans were very good at conquest and at keeping the conquered peoples within the Empire. At least at the beginning, all male Roman citizens were conscripted (drafted) into the army. Although their strategies and forms of government were different depending on the times and locations, Roman citizenship was offered to conquered peoples, democratic forms of government were established, and men in conquered lands were also conscripted into the army. Roman power and republican administration brought a Pax Romana to the entire region - there was relative peace in the Western world for the first time. The Romans introduced and spread a common law everywhere they conquered. Nothing like this had happened before in human history.

The Romans were unabashed admirers of the Greeks. The Greeks had introduced freedom of thought, reasoning, logic, science, individualism, and democracy. The Romans were excellent students. They studied the Greek teachings and learned to apply them better than the Greeks. The Romans built edifices, roads, and aqueducts, some of which remain today. The Romans even copied the art and religion of the Greeks. Many Roman statues are nearly identical with those of the Greeks. They also adopted the Greek gods but re-named them: Poseidon became Neptune, Hermes became Mercury, Ares became Mars, Hades became Pluto, Aphrodite became Venus, etc.

> *The Greeks were the architects of Western Civilization; the Romans were the builders. The Greeks accomplished the intellectual work of developing reasoning, the rules of logic and science, and democracy. The Romans successfully developed and spread the fruits of the Greek revolution through a wide portion of the known world. Left brain leadership of Western Civilization was at its peak.*

Beginning of the Common Era – the Year Zero

As the Common Era began, the Roman Republic was near its peak. The Romans had used the reasoning and deductive powers introduced by the Greeks and had accomplished a civilization prowess never before seen or even imagined in human history. Harnessing human thought was very powerful.

It is very appropriate that we began re-numbering our years at the date we now number zero. The events of that time were profound and continue to play a significant role in Western Civilization. Left brain control of Western Civilization began to falter as democracy ended and control of Western Civilization shifted from the group to the individual.

Two major events happened very near the year zero. These events eventually lead to the Dark Ages. The primary players in these two events had the same initials: Julius Caesar and Jesus Christ.

The weight of the immense land area that had been conquered began to cause cracks in the empire. The autonomy of local regions and the loyalties of the various armies, which were conscripted from local regions, were decentralizing forces. Local military power and rule became increasingly influential, making it more difficult to hold the Republic and empire together.

In 49 BCE, Julius Caesar returned from successful military campaigns in Africa, Spain, and Egypt and used his army to invade Rome. Although he crushed his enemies with force, he used political influence within the Senate to have himself appointed dictator for life. Julius Caesar was famously murdered in 44 BCE, but he had set the wheels in motion that led to the end of democracy in Rome - the end of the Roman Republic. By the end of his successor's reign, Caesar Augustus in 14 CE, the Republic had ended; henceforth, Emperors ruled Rome. Although this change is often cited as the beginning of the end for Rome, the Roman Empire actually reached its apex of territorial size, wealth, and peace during the first and second centuries CE under guidance of benevolent dictators.

The actions of Julius Caesar led to the fall of democracy and the beginning of rule by emperors, or individual people. The Roman Republic became the Roman Empire.

Julius Caesar should be given neither full credit nor full blame for this occurrence. Yes, he certainly triggered the events that caused the death of democracy in Rome. However, the Roman Republic was already under large strain to manage the burgeoning territory. There was a less-than-perfect implementation of democracy anyway - especially in other regions of the territory. But, the fact remains that democracy ended and rule by emperors was implemented.

The loss of democracy in Rome essentially broke the only right-brain participation in control of civilization and human destiny. (Discussed later)

From end of the second century CE until the fifth century CE, the Roman Empire continued but faced numerous threats both from within and without. This period of time also saw the most opulent style of living ever in Rome. During these times the Romans had particular problems with the northern (Germanic) and eastern (Huns and Goths) frontiers. Decay from within left Rome vulnerable. The Goths came from central Asia and first sacked Rome in 410 CE. By 500 CE nearly all remnants of the Western Roman Empire had been destroyed, although an eastern branch of the Roman Empire continued in some form for a couple more centuries.

The Huns and the Goths have been labeled barbarians because they spoke a crude language, were unable to read or write, and did not apparently understand agriculture. Their strengths were that they were well-trained and ruthless fighters who were also excellent horsemen. The luxury, corruption, and civil strife within Rome made them an easy target for the barbarians.

Christianity and Rome

Jesus was born into a time when the Roman Empire was near its peak of glory. Jesus was born in a location on the edge of the empire. This fringe area is where the clash of civilizations would have been most noticeable. This was a good vantage point from which to observe, feel, and analyze the effects of the Greco-Roman left brain civilizations that had dominated the Western world. The issues were at their clearest here.

Jesus was steeped in the Jewish tradition and was well-studied and strongly versed in the monotheistic God of the Old Testament. At almost exactly the same time as Jesus' ministry, the Romans ended 80 years of

Jewish autonomy. The Jewish people were outraged. The Jewish people had a pact with their God that they were to have their promised land, and now it had been taken from them by the Greco-Roman civilization. It had been taken from them by a civilization in which humans were in control, not God.

Jesus' background, and time and location of birth, enabled him to directly experience the effects of allowing human reasoning to control the destiny of humans. He experienced the effects of allowing the left brain, for the first time in human history, to take a lead in human group behavior and organization. Jesus was a strong believer in a monotheistic God - and therefore fundamentally came from a right-brain view of human grouping.

The events of the life of Jesus, during the years now numbered 30 to 33 CE, were not of great consequence to Rome at the time given the scope of their Empire. However, the rise of Christianity subsequent to Jesus' death would become central to the future of Rome and of Western Civilization.

Jesus Christ planted the seeds that brought the right brain back into control of Western Civilization. Jesus Christ taught about a monotheistic God that was loving and compassionate–and to be saved, one only needed to believe. Belief is a right-brain cognitive ability.

It was time for the right-brain "group" to re-assert its leadership position; the left brain was not succeeding. It was time for the survival mode of the right brain to again dominate human groups in the regions we now call "Western".

During the first and second century CE, Christianity spread quite widely, although it was not accepted by the Romans and many Christians were persecuted. By the end of the third century CE, approximately one in 10 of the Empire population was Christian, at least one Roman emperor had been Christian, and Christians were generally no longer persecuted. Diocletian ordered the last large scale Christian persecutions in 304-305 CE.

Constantine, who was the subsequent Roman emperor from 312 to 337 CE, made Christianity the official religion of the Roman Empire. During his reign, Christianity became part of the fabric of Roman rule. This had an immense impact upon the subsequent world, because it meant that the Roman world was Christian when it was destroyed. Many people at the time and many subsequent scholars blame Christianity for the fall of Rome. The writings of St. Augustine defended Christianity against those charges.

St. Augustine lived from 354 CE to 430 CE. He was a priest in the waning days of the Roman Empire, after Constantine, and hence, during the time that the Roman Empire had become Christian. His most famous and influential work was *The City of God.* The primary reason for this work was to defend Christianity against the claims that it was responsible for the decline of the Roman Empire during his time.

In his book, St. Augustine showed how two "cities" had fought with one another during world history. One city was of man and included the flesh and earthly materials; the other city was of God and not of this earth. The City of God was inside each Christian. Rome and the empire were part of the City of Man, and were separate from the City of God that was attainable by belief in Jesus. Ultimately, any glory found in the City of Man paled in comparison to the glory available to any believer in the City of God.

St. Augustine was a perceptive observer and a talented writer: he was also located at a transitional time and location. His observations and writings can be compared to those of Plato - who was also at a unique transitional time and location in human history. While Plato wrote at the time of left-brain emergence in human group control, St. Augustine wrote at the time of the demise of left-brain group control.

St. Augustine provided a clear distinction between the right brain (City of God) and the left brain (City of Man). The history of man certainly was a struggle between two worlds - that of the right brain and that of the left brain. The right brain cannot be completely analyzed and known - ultimately we can only "believe" in God. The City of God, or right brain, cannot ultimately be known by man's reasoning and logic which come from the left brain. The great accomplishments of the Roman Empire were those of the City of Man – i.e., the accomplishments of the left brain.

Christianity played an extremely large role during the fall of the Roman Empire and also during the Dark Ages that followed. The Roman elite had opulent lives. They placed materialism (the City of Man) and pleasures of the flesh ahead of all else. The same easy assimilation of individual contributions to the group that had helped to fuel the Greco-Roman civilization had also enabled individual self-desires, unchecked by group democracy, to easily and effectively corrupt the group.

The loss of democracy had led to abuses by man. Christianity, on the other hand, taught people to be satisfied with whatever they had in the way of earthly pleasures; the pleasures of the City of God that awaited them in the after-life were of overwhelming importance. This was the form of Christianity that ruled group organization as Western Civilization entered the Dark Ages.

After the Fall of Rome - Darkness

The Roman Empire had dominated Western Civilization for over a thousand years and, when it died, the vacuum created by the void was immense. There was no longer a central authority to manage larger groups of people, to manage the economy, or to build and maintain infrastructure. There was no longer a common law. When the only central authority died, the population dispersed into small groups.

The period from about 450 CE to 1000 CE is often referred to as the Dark Ages. This is for two reasons: life during those ages was very bleak; and there are few written records of the period.

During the Dark Ages, most of the classical Greek and Roman knowledge was lost. Daily living was largely reduced to survival. When the Roman Empire finally collapsed, it left a huge gap in authority. During the Dark Ages there was little organization to human groups. The only centralizing factor during these times was the Christian church. Unfortunately for this situation, the Christian church was probably the first religion that did not develop with a secular role of governance. The Church was unprepared to govern people - only to nurture their souls. During these times of mixed religious/state power, local leaders often misused their church-ordained power for personal gain.

Western Civilization had devolved to numerous small, localized, religious communities which were controlled by local fiefdoms that ruled by might. The common Christian God was essentially all that remained from the Roman center.

With the lack of central authority and the organization it had previously provided, the comforts of life were lost. Survival became a way of life. Even the many large and functional Roman buildings, roads and aqueducts were pilfered for their materials. The widespread adherence to the common laws that the Roman Empire provided no longer existed - lawlessness ruled. Personal protection became important - but it also became expensive as feudal lords provided protection for high prices.

Because of the lack of written materials, we cannot really know the state of mind of people during the Dark Ages. Judging from our vantage point in history and from our socio-economic position, it is easy to conclude that life was quite miserable. However, it is possible that many people, buoyed by Christian beliefs, were quite happy. They may have been happy with a very simple life and with time to praise the glory of God and wait for the second coming. Religion can work well to provide happiness in low-resource conditions.

During the Dark Ages, the right brain controlled human groups in the Western world.

THE LOSS OF DEMOCRACY AND RETURN OF THE RIGHT BRAIN IN THE DARK AGES

Christianity moved to the forefront of the Roman dictatorships (emperors) as the Empire went through its declining years and it can be argued that the church contributed to or even caused the decline. Religion and autocratic control of state have historically gone hand-in-hand and the mixing of Christian and state leadership in the latter Roman emperors certainly offered opportunity for either misuse or bad decisions in such concentration of power.

Christianity also helped people to survive and cope within the world of the Dark Ages in which the Western Civilization built by the left brain had been destroyed. The Dark Ages were characterized by small religious communities and by fiefdoms that controlled small regions based upon the use of might. This was essentially a return to some of the earliest days of human groupings after we had developed agriculture and animal domestication.

Regardless the role of religion (Christianity) in causing the fall of the Roman Empire, it appears quite clear that the right brain, and not the left brain, was in control of Western Civilization during the Dark Ages.

Democracy seems a necessary complement to allowing human reasoning to play a major role in human governance and destiny. Democracy allows the right and left brain to share in group decisions. People cast votes using both their left and right brains. Democracy can be viewed as the human (left brain) bargain made with our right brain. When that bargain was broken, the right brain took control....as is probably always its option. The greatest continuing danger to the West is that it will cast itself too far from the right brain.

In times of stress, survival trumps success. In times of stress, the right brain will wrest control from the left brain, on both the individual and group levels. Figure 19 shows how the collective human mind was organized during the hey-days of the Greeks and Romans - with the left brain largely in control of our groups. Figure 14 shows the collective mind during the Dark Ages. Effectively, group management returned to the right brain control of early human groupings.

Gnosticism

Christianity may bear Jesus' name, but the teachings of Christianity were very significantly developed and influenced by the leaders of the church in the years after Jesus' death. Church leaders selected the 27 books that were canonized in the New Testament after Christ's death and thereby selected the teachings of Christianity. However, these 27 books represent only a portion of early Christian literature, illustrated by the 1945 discovery of early Christian literature found in a vase at Nag Hammadi in Egypt and reported upon by Elaine Pagels in *The Gnostic Gospels.*

The official teachings of both orthodox Jews and Christians state that there is a chasm between god and man and that the world of god is unknowable to man except by belief. The teachings accepted into the New Testament of the Bible by the priests are consistent with this message. It is tempting to think that the inclusion decisions made by the priests of the Christian church were self-serving.

However, the Nag Hammadi documents, which were not accepted into the New Testament, contradict this message. These writings suggest that self-knowledge obtained through human reason is the same as knowledge of God. They state that we can know God through reason and self-inspection; the worlds of God and man intersect and are not completely separate from one another. These views were suppressed in the Christian beliefs, thus permanently separating the worlds of man and God for future generations, extending even to today. According to Christian beliefs, human reasoning cannot approach or know about God--it is by belief alone that we can know God. This very effectively took the world of God away from the left brain and gave it totally to the domain of the right brain from which it had come.

> *Imagine how different the history of Western Civilization might have been if the Gnostic point of view had been incorporated into Christianity. It would have given the left brain some input into religion. It would have given us the opportunity to use left-brain logic and reason to study the human core and the God and religion that are contained therein.*

The left brain begins to re-emerge

The years from 1000 to 1500 saw a slow but gradual re-emergence of some centers of civilization. There was some re-emergence of Greek thought and literature, but the Christian church was so strong that such thought was kept underground for fear of personal torture and/or death. Noted scholars who fit this label were Peter Abelard and St. Thomas Aquinas - both of whom were publicly reprimanded for viewpoints that slanted Church teachings in the direction of the participation of human thought.

In 1095 Pope Urban II launched the first of eight crusades that were to span a period of almost 200 years. The primary goal of these crusades was to recapture the Holy Land (specifically Jerusalem) from the hands of Islam. Only the first crusade was successful at gaining control of Jerusalem; the control lasted for 70 years. All of the other crusades ended in failure to capture Jerusalem. These crusades were fueled by the religious fervor of Christians to spread the word of their God.

Late in the Dark Ages, Peter Abelard and St. Thomas Aquinas espoused views that human reason could be applied to the study of God. This was an idea espoused by the Gnostics. In effect, this was a proposal to join the two Cities of St. Augustine. They suggested a connection between the City of Man and the City of God - or that the left brain participate in the study of God and religion.

The control of Western Civilization had been wrested from the left brain by the right brain in the form of Christianity for 1,000 years, ending with the Renaissance in 1,300. This period included the darkest years of Western Civilization. With the Renaissance, left-brain human reasoning and freedom of thought which had been introduced by the Greeks and then taken away during the Dark Ages, were again participating in Western Civilization.

Renaissance

By 1300, the approximate starting date of the Renaissance, Western Civilization groups had been led by right brain beliefs for about 1,000 years, and the results for human material comfort on earth had not been good.

The reasoning and logic of the left brain re-emerged in the Renaissance to guide Western Civilization. The original works of the Greeks were rediscovered and a new age of reason began. Today we see the fruits of that Renaissance. Control of Western Civilization was returned to the left brain; science and democracy were reinstituted. The right and left partnership was re-established.

The Renaissance was a truly amazing period that ran for several centuries. The reason and logic of man again took control of Western Civilization, reflecting renewed leadership by the left brain. Literature and the arts began to flourish. People, and not just religious figures, begin to dominate the subject of paintings. People became the focus of activities; no longer were all activities centered on God and religion. Perspective appeared in our art as we learned how to better represent the world around us.

Many of the classic Greek writings were rediscovered. Reasoning and logic were again examined and became drivers of civilization. Dissemination of knowledge among people was greatly enhanced with invention of the printing press by Gutenberg. Famous Renaissance writers include: Dante Alighieri, John Milton, Francois Rabelais, Geoffrey Chaucer, William Shakespeare, Thomas More, and Miguel de Cervantes.

Science blossomed as left brain reason and logic were applied to study of the world. Academic institutions proliferated and journals of scientific findings were published. The names of great scientists of the Renaissance include: Leonardo da Vinci, Nicholas Copernicus, Galileo Galilei, Isaac Newton, and Renee Descartes.

In the sixteenth century national states began to form, including France, England, Spain and Germany. These were monarchies ruled by royalty that served at the pleasure of God. In many cases the rulers were despotic. However, they usually were able to at least convince their subjects that they were benevolent, and times were good enough that they could get away with self-indulgence. An infrastructure of roads, buildings and ships was developed after many centuries without. The monarchies supported exploration, primarily for the riches it could bring. Famous explorers included Marco Polo, Christopher Columbus, and Ferdinand Magellan.

The Christian church had mixed reactions to the Renaissance. During medieval times many local church leaders used the church for personal gain and power, so this genre of people had no difficulties accepting the new prominence of human reason. True church people, however, struggled with the conflict between human desires and godliness. Notable church leaders were Desiderius Erasmus and Martin Luther. Church reform was occurring.

Two types of revolutions began in England in the 17th and 18th centuries. The first was the Industrial Revolution generally defined as the use of machines in the manufacture of products. The second was a political revolution, replacing monarchy with a representative and democratic government.

> *For nearly 1,000 years people within Western Civilization had relegated responsibility for their lives to the church. They believed this was the best thing to do for themselves and certainly for their souls. This period was characterized by a near disappearance of Greco-Roman civilization. With advent of the Renaissance, people began to take control of their destiny again.*

The American Revolution

The American Revolution, from British rule, in 1776 played a very significant role in the development of our Western Civilization. The names Thomas Jefferson, Alexander Hamilton, George Washington, and Benjamin Franklin must be included among the leaders of Western Civilization.

The American Revolution allowed the continued development of Western Civilization in a new nation with unspoiled lands. A democratic form of government, seeded by England, and not monarchy emerged as the form of government. Also, since America had been a colony and rebelled against being so, America's leaders did not immediately follow the imperialistic ways of the European powers. America was founded on a strong set of democratic principles and a guaranteed set of personal freedoms and rights.

The Triumvirate of Western Civilization

The triumvirate of science, capitalism and democracy currently leads Western Civilization as a collective surrogate for the usual and classic role of religion.

In Western Civilization science is taken to be the truth; capitalism is the primary method by which we conduct our work and allocate resources; and democracy is our governmental structure. All three work in a system of checks, balances, and cooperation not unlike the judiciary, legislative and executive branches of the US government. The American Revolution is largely responsible for setting up the relationships between capitalism and democracy - science has taken on a life of its own and has become integrated with the other two. The world is currently experiencing and reaping benefits from the U.S.-lead Western Civilization - the current pinnacle of human ability to harness the planet's resources to our benefit.

Science is responsible for exploring and answering questions about the "world". Science is guided by search for the truth about nature. Science is like the judiciary - it is largely independent of outside influence. Neither capitalism nor democracy exerts much control, if any, over the direction of science. Science is driven to reveal the truth about nature. Capitalism does not innately care about the truth. Science is also largely not guided by democracy - science is not necessarily democratic. The truth must be and is its guiding principle. Science is largely independent of control by capitalism or democracy. However, the amount of scientific inquiry is influenced by both capitalism and democracy, because most science is dependent upon either business or government for its funding.

Capitalism[3] is characterized by creating a free and open market so that efforts, goods and pleasure can be properly valued and exchanged. However, capitalism has no inherent sense of truth, fairness, or morality. Capitalism is good at developing the truths discovered by science and implementing them for group development. Capitalism is a tool that,

3 Capitalism n: an economic system characterized by private or corporate ownership of capital goods, by investments that are determined by private decision rather than by state control, and by prices, production and the distribution of goods that are determined mainly in a free market.

when properly used, can very effectively harness the resources of the planet for group and individual economic success. By its very nature, capitalism creates competition among individuals and can, therefore, create disharmony among people. Capitalism must be properly controlled by democracy to make sure it does not transgress that which is fair to individuals. Capitalism is largely driven by satisfaction of individual self-desires.

Democracy[4] is our form of government and is the foundational structure for group in Western Civilization. Democracy structures groups with governmental framework and with the controls it exerts over capitalism. Democracy establishes rules and alters capitalistic exchange values when needed for the good of the people. Democracy does not usually (and should not) meddle in science, but should provide an environment for the advancement of science.

Science and capitalism are both functions of our left brain. Democracy, by letting individuals vote their preferences, includes input from both the left-brain reasoning and right-rain feelings. Democracy is the only right-brain group contribution in the triumvirate of Western Civilization.

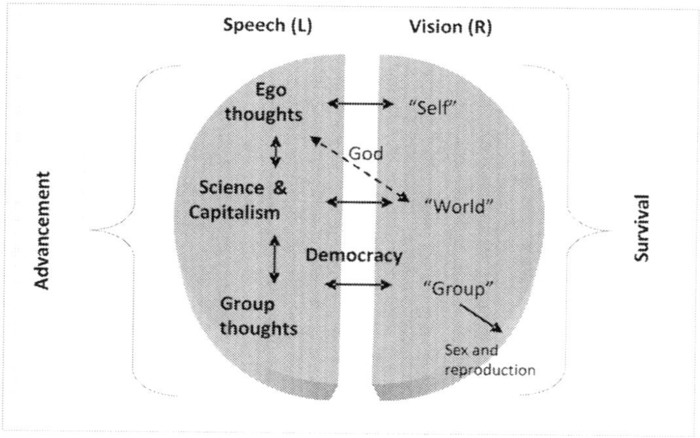

Figure 20. *The current Western Civilization Sensory Mind, showing addition of capitalism to the earlier Greek diagram.*

4 Democracy n: a government in which the supreme power is vested in the people and exercised by them directly or indirectly through a system of representation.

Summary

Western Civilization is a unique form of civilization in which religion plays little role in societal governance. By this characteristic alone, it is highly unusual compared to previous and other current civilizations. Instead, Western Civilization is primarily based upon three institutions: science, capitalism, and democracy that work together in a system of checks and balances. Western Civilization has strong roots in the Judeo-Christian God, but religion currently serves as a conscience rather than a central role.

East and West

There are significant differences between Eastern and Western cultures and philosophies. The social structures, attitudes of individuals and groups, philosophies, and many other characteristics are observably different between East and West.

> *Western and Eastern Civilizations, largely built on Socrates/Plato and Buddha/Confucius respectively, have fundamental differences in group structure. The differences in group structure represent different arrangements of the collective sensory mind (Figures 20 and 21).*

Nisbett (2003) provides a thorough analysis of these differences. Some of the main differences are summarized in the Table below. Nisbett and I each acknowledge that these broad stroke statements about differences overlook the many individual cultural and sub-cultural differences that exist in the world. Broad categorization is not done in any way to slight those differences, rather to point out the large and fairly uniform differences that exist between East and West. Nisbett defines the East to include China and the eastern Asian countries with strong Chinese influence; the West includes Western Europe. For our purposes here, I include the Americas in the West and, because of similarities between Buddhist and Confucian philosophy, India is included in the East.

Table 1. *Fundamental differences between East and West*

	EAST	WEST
Sense of self	Weak	Strong
Sense of dependence on group	Strong	Weak
Attitude and focus	Holistic (visual)	Analytical and detailed (verbal)
Life control	The world is complex and we have poor control over events.	The world operates by rules and can be analyzed and controlled
Universal God?	No, there is a universal truth	Yes
Ultimate truth	Universal, Nature, ultimately can't be known	Analyzed by science, can be attained
Left/Right brain orientation	Right	Left
Left brain "success"	Advancement	Attain harmony and enlightenment
Visual attention	Background seen first	Foreground seen first

These differences between East and West go back to the fundamental differences in the manner in which the "thought" leaders of the Axis Age helped to construct the relationships between our individual and collective right and left minds. More than a billion people today can claim civilization heritage from the Greeks (including the Americas), more than a billion can claim civilization heritage from Buddha and Hinduism, and more than two billion can claim civilization heritage from ancient China and Confucius. These civilizations have different rulebooks on life. Diagrams of the Western and Eastern Sensory Minds are shown in Figures 20 and 21 respectively.

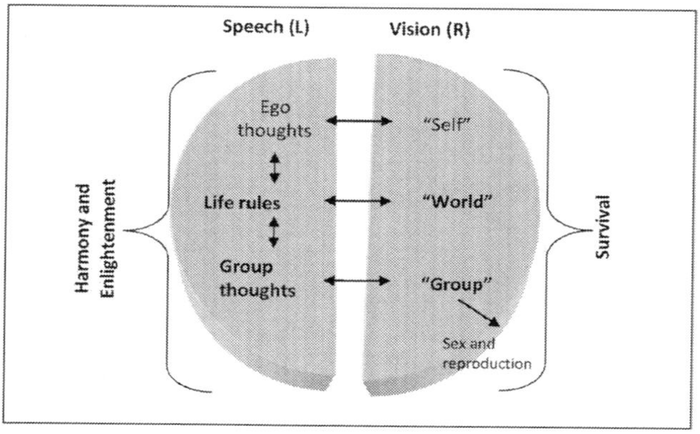

Figure 21. *The Eastern Sensory Mind. The Eastern mind is strongly oriented towards the concept of the "**world**" located in our right brain. It also emphasizes **group** over individual and the objectives of the left brain are the attainment of harmony and enlightenment. These are defined in terms of attaining harmony with the right-brain concept of the world.*

Both the Buddhist and Confucian teachings emphasize the existence of an ultimate life or truth associated with the "world". This ultimate truth is that to which individuals and groups should strive. It is like a guiding light. However, it cannot be well-defined and is something that we feel. This is because it comes from our vision-based (right brain) cognition. It is word-less. The ultimate truth or life is essentially the same wonderment the first humans had about the world around them. This strongly anchors the Eastern world view in the vision-based right brain.

By contrast, the Western Mind is oriented towards science, or the left-brain analysis of the world around us. Although the Western Mind acknowledges the many unknowns about the world, those unknowns are not viewed as the ultimate truth to which we orient ourselves. The unknowns are generally viewed as aspects of the world that science has not yet analyzed or been able to figure out. The West trusts science as the arbiter of truth about the world; thereby, strongly anchoring the world view in the left brain.

Another major difference between the Eastern and Western minds is the definition of success towards which the left brain strives. The West is driven by advancing the civilization. This is accomplished largely through science and technology and increasing our abilities to utilize the world in order to gain greater comfort and satisfaction for individuals. The West is driven by Gross Domestic Product (GDP). The Eastern Mind, on the other hand, defines success in terms of attaining harmony and enlightenment. Harmony and enlightenment are attained by approaching or attaining the truth about life. The Western objective is based upon the activities of the left brain and individual comfort and satisfaction. The Eastern objective is based on attaining human orientation towards the right brain truths about "life".

Another East-West difference is the orientation towards group or self. Eastern philosophy emphasizes the responsibilities of the individual towards the group; whereas, the Western mind is oriented towards the self or ego of the individual. The Eastern orientation towards the group works well towards the objective of attaining group harmony. The Western orientation leads towards greater agitation between individuals and stresses competition. The Western emphasis on the individual also provides greater opportunity for individual contributions and supports the objective of advancement.

Nisbett states: "My research has led me to the conviction that two utterly different approaches to the world have maintained themselves for thousands of years. These approaches include profoundly different social relations, views about the nature of the world, and characteristic thought processes." These differences between the Eastern and Western minds are fundamental. Due to the fundamental and lasting effects of the Axis Age leaders, clear distinctions are easily observed even today - 2,500 years after their formations.

Of course, these are generalities. Also, the peoples and nations of the world are changing. In fact, the recent advances in international travel and communication have significantly resulted in inter-mixing of these cultural philosophies. Most of the change has involved infusion of Western Civilization into Eastern countries such as India and China. This is mostly because the West has been so successful at using the left brain to harness the resources of the planet to improve human comfort. Eastern countries are appreciating and choosing comfort over enlightenment. These situations will be discussed later.

CHAPTER 9

WHERE ARE WE NOW?

CIVILIZATION – LOOK AROUND YOU!

Look around you. Are you as amazed as I by all of the things around us? Buildings, refrigerators, the computer I'm currently using, music from a radio, the ceramic mug from which I drink tea from China - these are all provided by of our current civilization. Civilization is a product of the collective efforts of humans. It is testament to our cooperation with one another. Without such cooperative efforts, we would not have all of this. Frankly, I could not even make the chair in which I sit were it up to my individual efforts. Our civilization is truly amazing - as have been past civilizations.

Civilization is the grandest expression of our left-brain group-think abilities. The foundation, however, of our groups and civilizations is based in our right-brain sense of group that comes from the visual mind and animal world.

Civilization is a strange thing. It is totally created by and dependent upon humans, yet much of it is inanimate and exists outside each of us. A large part of civilization is also inside each of us - witness the rules, ethics and behavioral patterns by which we interact with one another. Another interesting aspect of civilization is that it endures beyond the life of each individual. Civilization continues as a part of the species despite the fact that individual humans are each part of it (and contribute to it) for a relatively short and finite period of time. In many respects, civilization is a better definition of the human species than is any single human being.

And, yes, civilization does advance. Oh my - how it advances! Today we witness advances in civilization on a daily basis: new electronic implementations, cell phones, advanced medical treatments, biotechnology, the worldwide web, and space travel. My generation has witnessed (or developed) all of the above in addition to landing on our moon, development of the inter-state highway system, air travel that is accessible to most people, color television, personal computers, HD TV, and amazing medical advances that enable us to live healthier and longer. The previous generation witnessed (and developed) refrigeration, nuclear bombs, jet travel, and television. The generation before that witnessed (and developed) the first automobile and first air flight; the generation before that witnessed (and developed) the first harnessing of electricity and the light bulb; and the generation before that contributed the Industrial Revolution, and before that…on and on.

It has been said that, "We stand on the shoulders of giants who have gone before us." My only issue with the statement is that nearly every person's shoulders are used to help others - not just the giants. That being said, however, standing on the shoulders of those who have gone before us is precisely how civilization is built. We are all still standing on the shoulders of the unknown person who invented the wheel. But, once it was invented, it became part of civilization and all future generations were able to use it. The same is true about the first humans who domesticated plants to create crops of food, those who created the first alphabet, the Greek philosophers, Alhazen and mathematical principles, Newton's understanding of light and color, Galileo's understanding of gravity, astronomy and the universe; Descartes and his structural description of the world, Gutenberg and the printing press; the Wright brothers and air flight; Edison and the light bulb and phonograph; and the Beatles, Barbara Streisand, Versace, and Madonna for music and style. The list of giants is larger than any encyclopedia.

Today, children ride toys with wheels at the age of 18 months. When they begin speaking, part of the rules they are taught are Greek logic. They learn on computers by age three, and even Einstein's theory of relativity is taught in grade school science. The contributions of giants are incorporated into the base knowledge and experience of most humans - and they become part of civilization.

> *Civilization is built by standing on the shoulders of those who have gone before us. Our group-think abilities have been cumulative and built upon the thinking and contributions of those who have gone before us. This has enabled us to conquer the planet.*

Humans today have a much greater knowledge base and understanding of the world around us than any previous generation of humans - but does that mean that we have a greater mental capacity than those who have gone before us? There is considerable scientific debate about brain evolution. It is possible that our brains are anatomically and/or physiologically more advanced than those who preceded us by 100,000 years (first *Homo sapiens*), 60,000 years (first art) or even by 12,000 years (first agriculture). However, the advances of civilization we are witnessing within recent generations are occurring much faster than brain evolution can occur. This suggests that most of the advances are due to collective knowledge of civilization and not necessarily due to evolutionary changes in the brain. Because humans continually build on the contributions of previous generations, each generation benefits from those previous discoveries and cumulative knowledge. Each generation inherits a higher level of civilization - the base level of knowledge and understanding continually increases from one generation to the next.

It would also be completely unfair to list only the "giants" as contributors to the advance of civilization. Do not most of us stand on the shoulders of our parents? We rely and depend on them to introduce, train, and educate us to the contemporary civilization around us. And, how about our school teachers? The librarian who helps us select the correct written materials? The car mechanic who keeps our automobile running so that we can continue going to work? The doctor who heals us so that we can continue our own personal contributions? Or the entertainer who puts a smile on our face so that life has more meaning?

It is not only the "giants" that have contributed to civilization–most people contribute in some way to civilization.

We truly do stand on the shoulders of those who have gone before us. Civilization is much like an enduring structure that each of us inherits - a birthright in life. But we not only inherit it–we also each add to it. Each of us is part of the *collective group think*. We each have it within us.

There is a civilization that continues and grows beyond each and every one of our lives. Civilization is a product of human beings. It is dependent upon human beings en masse, but not dependent upon any single human being. There is something very strong and powerful that connects humans with one another and enables us to work together and contribute above and beyond the contributions of past generations in order to continue the advancement of Civilization. It is truly amazing that this happens despite the life and death of all the millions of individual humans who contribute to it. Civilization endures from generation to generation and is truly a product of human beings as a whole - but it also relies upon our individual contributions.

Civilization is a result of our left-brain group think, which sits atop our strong sense of "group" embedded in the right brain.

Humans: Current Status

The advancement of humans and our civilizations has been truly amazing. We can see it in our lifetimes. The first emergence of our human ancestors from the apes was approximately six million years ago. If we treat the entire human period of development as a 24 hour day beginning at midnight, we do not see the first use of hand held tools until 2 p.m.–14 hours of relative inactivity in human development. There is another long period of time until we see the first emergence of *Homo sapiens*–not until 11:36 p.m.–only 24 minutes left in the day. But, then the pace quickens.

With only two minutes 24 seconds left in the day, we see the earliest signs of agriculture, with one minute 12 seconds left we see the first major civilizations such as Egypt. The American Revolution occurs with only three seconds left in the day. The very last second before the stroke of midnight sees humans develop electricity, cars, planes and computers. The pace at the end of the day is dizzying.

Mithen creatively likens man's development to a play with acts and scenes. He describes the final (and current) scene as follows:

> *"As soon as the third scene of Act 4 begins, we see people in the Near East planting crops, and then domesticating animals. Events now flash past at bewildering speed. People create towns, and then cities. A succession of empires rise and fall and the props become ever more dominant, diverse and complex: in no more than an instant, carts have become cars and writing tablets word processors. After almost six million years of relative inaction, we find it difficult to make sense of this final hectic scene."*

The current advancement of human civilizations is truly phenomenal - almost beyond comprehension. One of the earliest major technology revolutions in our history was the development of agriculture, which resulted in periodic doubling of our food production, and likewise, freed our time to perform other tasks that helped advance the group. Today we have overlapping technology revolutions. Look at the current advances in computer inter-connectivity, information flow, voice communication (cell phone), advances in medical care, and advanced manufacturing techniques. Each of these interacts with the others to result in exponential growth of our civilization.

Human groups have evolved from small groups of hunter/gatherers, to small agricultural communities, to towns, cities, and nations. Each increase in the group size required a more sophisticated social organization - one that could both serve and hold together large numbers of humans. Western Civilization has a social organization that is unique in its ability to utilize both the right and left brains to fulfill group success.

The civilization we have developed is amazingly complex. Have you ever wondered how it all holds together? I am continuously amazed that our systems of government regulations, company rules, wage structure, natural resources utilization, manufacturing capability, taxes, forms, machinery, food production, scheduling, entertainment, etc., actually "works". Think about what you and others that you know do in a typical day. How is it all orchestrated to work in harmony? Water comes from my faucet, electricity from the wall socket, and clothes in my size are readily available in numerous stores. I have a laundry machine to clean them, a newspaper is delivered to me each day, I can rely on TV news precisely at 6:30 p.m. each day. My car starts when I turn the key, fuel is readily available when I need it, I can address a letter and it will be delivered anywhere in the world, and I can send an e-mail message to anyone almost instantaneously. How does this all work?

We are each highly dependent upon one another, but it is "organized" through our systems of commerce, business, social organizations, etc., such that we don't usually think about it or even realize it.

The individual contributions of each person are very well-coordinated by our systems. Each person goes through their week and contributes to the whole by way of the job they perform along with their other daily activities that contribute to the health, welfare and/or general well-being of others in the group. We each largely proceed through our daily activities without even thinking about how inter-reliant we are, or that our individual activities are contributing to the benefit of the group. Also, when we think of "group", we are more likely to think about our department at work, the club to which we belong, our athletic team, our minority group, etc. We do not usually think of our group in terms of the civilization to which we each belong and contribute. However, we each definitely can feel the ties to our country and to our western civilization. I clearly recall my feelings and the outpouring of feelings from others on 9/11/2001. We each felt that we had been personally attacked.

We each are normally so consumed in our daily living that we typically don't think about or appreciate the wonders and accomplishments of our human groups.

Fundamental Differences in Current Human Civilizations

Homo sapiens are the most advanced life form on this planet. Our civilizations are the most fundamental organization of our species. Our mind is what has enabled us to be so successful, and all humans share the same basic sensory mind. Different civilizations have different organizations of the left/right and self/group aspects of the sensory mind.

There are clear and undeniable differences in current human civilizations. Although it is a clear over-simplification, at the grossest level the world civilizations can be divided into three: Western, Islamic, and Eastern. Their historical paths are shown in Figure 22.

The orientations of the Eastern, Western, and Islamic Civilizations are fundamentally different from one another. They are like different families with different base assumptions about human grouping behavior. Insofar as our species is concerned, they represent different mind strategies for the survival and, now, success of our species.

The West is generally oriented towards success and individualism. The East is generally oriented towards survival, group, and the truth about life. Islam is generally oriented towards a single God. Each of these is a different arrangement of the group sensory mind (Figures 20. 21, and 14 respectively).

The roots of Western Civilization come from the Greeks and their formal development and inclusion of the left brain in civilization guidance. Western Civilization was given a universal God at transition to the Dark

Ages. The West has an attachment to the God of Abraham, but the East does not.

The Islamic Civilization is directly descended from the God of Abraham and modified by Muhammad. The Islamic Civilization is still largely configured with God at the center. God and religion are held in very high esteem in Islamic countries; religion generally holds a higher role in Islamic states than does the political state. God is central to the Islamic civilization.

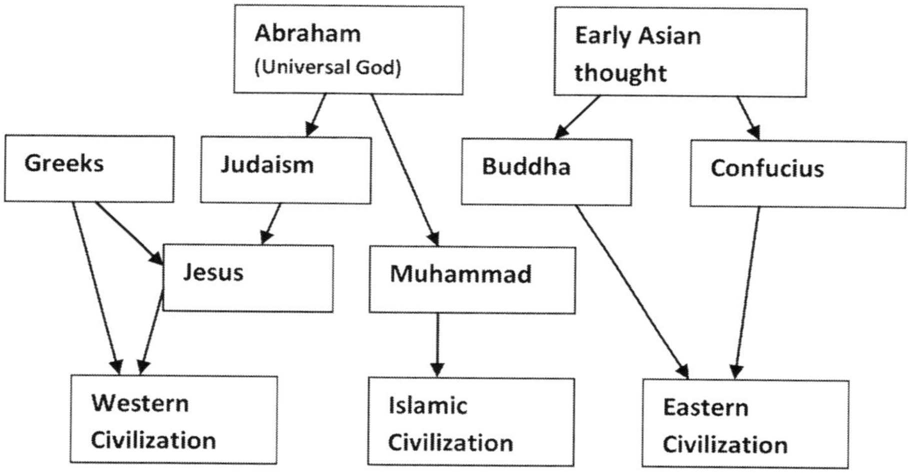

Figure 22. *The historical paths from which the three major civilizations on this planet are derived.*

The collective mind of the Islamic Civilization is organized essentially the same way as the earliest human groups. It is correct to state that Islam is fundamentalist. The diagrammatic representation is identical with the earliest forms of small-group gods shown in Figure 14.

> *The Eastern and Western Civilizations have significantly different orientations of the individuals towards self/group, and also towards thinking/feeling, as shown in Figure 23. The Thinking/Feeling orientation differences can also be characterized as different orientations towards the right or left brains.*

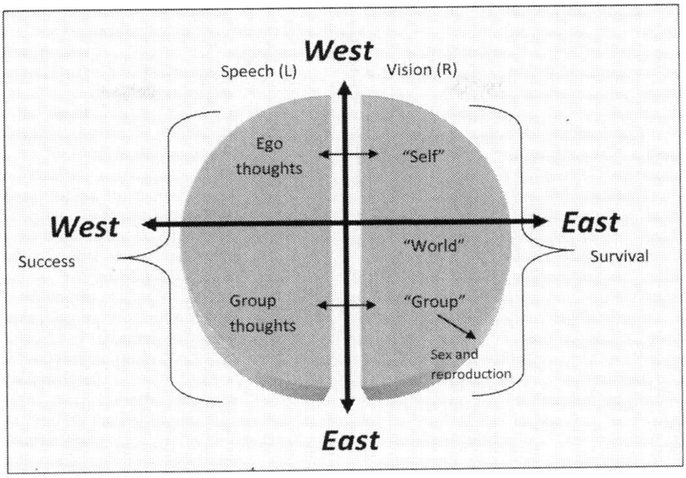

Figure 23. *Individuals within Western Civilizations are oriented more towards the Self and to the Thinking left brain, whereas individuals within Eastern Civilizations are oriented more towards the Group and towards the Feeling right brain.*

I feel it valid to view the current civilizations as being in a Darwinian survival struggle. Historically they have been engaged in an ebb and flow of dominance and inter-relationships with one another. Ultimately, the Darwinian struggle is for survival of our species. Humans no longer need be concerned about conquering life on this planet. That mission has been accomplished. Now our competitive and, unfortunately, war-like nature causes us to compete among our own species groups - sometimes leading us to fight.

The West, with its emphasis on the left brain and the self, has been the most capable at developing the planet's resources and also being aggressive to others. The East, with its emphasis on group and seeking truth in life, seems better at satisfying happiness and surviving with fewer resources. It appears that the availability of resources to be developed could swing the relative success of East vs. West. The West will likely continue to be successful so long as it can continue to creatively use and develop the planet's resources. The East, however, is better poised to survive if Western Civilization were to flounder. The Islamic Civilization seems to have yet another approach towards group organization. Their orientation towards God causes strong internal focus and resistance to outside influence. The Islamic Civilization may be optimally positioned for survival if resource development does not keep pace with population.

Now, questions about the future:

> *What is best for our species? Is it good for our species survival to concurrently have all three Civilization strategies? Does this give us better survivability by enabling us to cover a broader array of environmental and survival scenarios? Now that we have dominated this planet, what are the scenarios for our future existence and potential challenges to it? Is the collective left brain of our species able to actually think about the future scenarios and develop and implement a coordinated and logical plan for our future?*

There are many reasons to believe *Homo sapiens* are not able to think about and plan their future. It almost seems presumptuous and arrogant to think that our left brain is capable of altering or impacting our future survivability by planning and guiding. Developing and agreeing a plan seems beyond any current world organizations. And, we can't even agree on the direction of our own country, let alone the future of our species.

But, there are more reasons to believe we can think about and plan for our future. There is nothing unnatural about our left brain. After-all, it was developed by Life and it is natural to think that its abilities should be used as much as possible for Darwinian survival and success. The past 2,500 years also clearly demonstrate that left brain participation in group socio-political organization alters the course of *Homo sapiens.* The evidence appears to support that incorporation of our left-brain into group thinking has and continues to have an effect on survivability and success of our species. Furthermore, the following is an example that our left brain has already contributed to enhance future survivability of our species. Humans have given thought and developed plans to minimize or avert asteroid collision. This seems a clear demonstration that *Homo sapiens* left-brain thinking can plan for future survivability chances of *Homo sapiens.*

Western Civilization

Let us further analyze the current Western Civilization and how the right/left and self/group divisions of the sensory mind are incorporated into its structure.

Self/Group in Civilization

The self/group axis is fundamental to Darwinian survival and to the evolution of all advanced life on this planet. This includes all advanced species and to the individuals within species. The self/group orientation of individuals within a species is critical to the survival of the species. In the animal world, the self/group orientation of individuals within the species is based upon vision-based behavior and cognition. We humans have developed left-brain cognition that overlays our right brain self/group orientation.

Human bonding and individual contribution to the good of the group have been central tenets of human groups since our days as hunter-gatherers. As discussed earlier, there are two primary human needs that motivate humans:

- Self-desires–which are self-serving
- Group-responsibility–an inner need to contribute to the group - which is more altruistic

Which of these is the best motivator? Clearly we know some people who are very strongly motivated by making money for their own personal consumption. They do not seem very interested in the fate of their fellow humans, nor in the value of their contributions to the group. On the other hand, some people are "givers" and are primarily driven by the value that they bring to others and to society. Both of these needs operate simultaneously in most people - each person requiring a certain level of self-protection and comfort and each person also deriving meaning in life by a sense of worthiness that comes from contributing to others or to the whole. The balance can be different across individuals.

Human groups, including our civilizations, establish the norms for accepted self/group balance.

Self/Group in Western Civilization

Western Civilization stands on the pillars of capitalism, democracy, and science,. These collectively serve as surrogates for the classic role of god and religion in most previous and many current civilizations. How does this triumvirate meet our human needs and how does it motivate humans to contribute to group success in comparison to religious-based civilizations?

Capitalism and Democracy as Human Motivators

Capitalism operates through the medium of money - it places value upon and provides an exchange rate for human effort, pain and pleasure. Capitalism encourages group-responsibility behavior, but it is not guided by it. Capitalism, by itself, is not concerned with truth - this guidance comes from science; nor is it concerned with fairness - this guidance comes from democracy.

Capitalism is Darwinian insofar as it rewards the fittest - i.e., those who contribute the most to civilization. This is good for civilization. Capitalism uses money to compensate people for their contributions. Money is used to satisfy the needs for protection and comfort of the Ego.

Capitalism primarily motivates by satisfying the needs of our self-desires - not by satisfying our group-responsibility needs. Capitalism does not directly motivate us by our more noble and altruistic needs - but, instead, motivates us by our more selfish needs.

Ultimately, however, it is group success that is most important to the success of human beings. Capitalism has no protection mechanism for the comfort and safety of weaker individuals compared to stronger individuals. Capitalism does not motivate individuals according to the needs of the group. On the contrary, capitalism motivates according to meeting individual needs, not according to meeting the group needs (or, the will of god).

Does motivating humans by satisfying their self-interests, as capitalism does, serve the needs of the group?

Adam Smith (1723-1790), in his famous treatise "An Inquiry into the Nature and Causes of the Wealth of Nations", provided the theoretical construct for the free-market economy that is an integral part of capitalism. He argued that individual self-interest guides the most efficient use of resources and that the public good is best accomplished with a free market system. The application of these free-market theories has been wildly successful - resulting in the large success of our current Western Civilization. Capitalism has led our group success primarily by motivating individuals according to their self-desires.

Capitalism does serve the needs of the group. It does so by coordinating people who are individually motivated by self-interests. Through a free market the values of services and goods are determined by the value of each to the group. In this manner the needs of the group are satisfied and the rewards that people receive from them are likewise established. Ideally, those who bring the greatest value to the group also receive the largest personal rewards. It is a very clever system.

Democracy stands for fairness and equality for each person. Each person has input into the government and each person is also guaranteed certain freedoms. As such, democracy is a good counter balance to capitalism. One of the strengths of U.S. democracy is the two-party system. The Republican Party leans towards representing capitalism and the Democratic Party towards democracy and individual rights. The ebb and flow of power between the two parties allows for a healthy management of the balance between capitalism and democracy. The table below shows the alternation of power between Republican and Democrat. This flexibility in the system is necessary for our nation (especially as leader of Western Civilization) to deal with changing internal and external factors - much as a tree sways in the wind. However, it could be argued that the current balance of power between Republican and Democrat is so balanced as to be stale-mated.

With only one exception, due to the Carter presidency only being one term (four years), the U.S. has alternated between eight years of Republican and eight years of democratic presidency since World War II.

Democrat 8	Harry S Truman (1945-1953)
Republican 8	Dwight D. Eisenhower (1953-1961)
Democrat 8	John F. Kennedy (1961-1963) / Lyndon B. Johnson (1963-1969)
Republican 8	Richard Nixon (1969-1974) / Gerald Ford (1974-1977)
Democrat 4	Jimmy Carter (1977-1981)
Republican 12	Ronald Reagan (1981-1989) / George Bush (1989-1993)
Democrat 8	Bill Clinton (1993-2001)
Republican 8	George W. Bush (2001-2009)
Democrat ?	Barack Obama (2009-present)

The Cold War, which was "fought" for more than forty years from the end of World War II up until 1989 with the fall of the Berlin Wall, was a great struggle over two systems - effectively to determine which of the two competing systems was most successful. Capitalism had greater survival value and, in a Darwinian sense, "won".

The communist system concentrated on the individual worker. There was much less reliance on money as a motivator - people were generally compensated relatively equally and the primary motivator was the desire for success of the community. The economy and allocation of resources within it was largely planned by the government.

The communist system directly motivated people primarily on the basis of their altruistic and purer needs to contribute to the whole. Although it may be a sad commentary on humans, capitalism won out over purists who believe in altruism as a strong motivator.

Although capitalism motivates individuals according to their self-desires, and does not directly motivate according to the needs of the group, paired with democracy it was a more successful system than communism. Although the combination of capitalism and democracy won the Cold War, it does not mean there cannot be a better system. We must question whether this strategy is the appropriate one to carry *Homo sapiens* into our future.

SCIENCE AND RELIGION

In today's world of science we have very accurately described the external world - and continue to do so more fully and precisely. In the earliest civilizations and some current ones, god has guided man into the unknown. Is it possible that science can now take the place of god? Do we now know everything - or at least have the methodology (the scientific method) by which to know and understand everything? Science seems clever at answering many questions about the external world, but it will never reach the end of the questions.

It is also unlikely that science will ever be able to truly discover the essence of what it is to be human. Science will probably never be able to totally eliminate the need for belief in a higher truth such as god. It will certainly help to get us closer, but it will likely never provide a complete understanding of life. Science has probably never answered a question that did not also result in asking several new ones. The job of science will never be done.

In Western Civilization, religion (based upon god) and science have been in opposition to one another. However, this is largely because science has challenged and disputed several specific aspects of religious dogma - such as the creation. Religions have been inflexible in addressing such conflicts. These conflicts notwithstanding, god still plays a needed role in Western Civilization. Science will never be able to answer all of life's questions; and Western Civilization does not have the Eastern orientation towards seeking the right-brain truths about life. God, in Western Civilization, helps to maintain orientation towards the truths of life contained in the right brain.

There should not be a clash between science and god. God represents the very essence of life and what it is to be human; and science is simply the human method of investigating the world around us. We need them both.

Summary

Capitalism has very successfully motivated people according to self-desires. The results have been astounding in terms of material wealth and meeting self-serving desires. The free-market economy, as per Adam Smith, has been particularly clever at motivating individuals by self-desires in a way that their contributions are coordinated for phenomenal group success. Western Civilization has thrived because of this group success - nearly entirely attained by self-desire motivation.

Democracy structures our system for fairness and provides governance and justice. Democracy is a logical companion of the individualism of the Greeks. Even though it springs from individualism, by allowing each person a voice in group decisions and management, it also primarily meets the needs of the group. Although democracy does not serve as a primary motivator for people - it plays the role of an organizer.

Likewise, science is not a human motivator. Science largely serves as the ultimate arbiter of truth and, in this way, serves one of the roles of god and religion. However, one of the primary roles of religion has been to motivate behavior according to our group-responsibility. Science does not serve that role.

> *The triumvirate of Western Civilization (capitalism, democracy, and science) strongly motivates people according to self-desires (through capitalism), but does not directly motivate people by group-responsibility. The success of the group (Western Civilization) has been accomplished by a capitalistic and free-market system that coordinates the contributions of individuals who are each largely motivated by self-interests. Democracy serves the needs of the group, but even it is likely driven more by self-interest because that is how many voters make ballot decisions.*

On the other hand, the individual freedoms within Western Civilization certainly give individuals the choice to be motivated by group-responsibility to the extent that they desire. There is nearly complete freedom to pursue the higher-level satisfactions that derive from behavior motivated by group-responsibility. In our civilization we are each completely free to be motivated by our needs for group-responsibility and to derive the highest levels of self-satisfaction associated with meeting those needs.

> *In Western Civilization, group-responsibility is a direct individual human motivator only insofar as the satisfaction that individuals receive from such actions encourages such behavior. It is also possible that our success has provided us with greater opportunity to allow us to be guided by altruism.*

Civilization conflict

It may be easy for us to think of Western Civilization as the only valid one on this planet, but, of course, this is not true. Samuel Huntington, author of *The Clash of Civilization and the Remaking of the World Order*, points out that most civilizations view themselves as the center of the world. This seems particularly true of people in the United States who occupied a largely virgin territory that is geographically isolated in the world with no unfriendly borders.

Huntington identifies 8 major civilizations currently on our planet. Western, African, Sinic, Hindu, Islamic, Japanese, Latin American, and Orthodox. Although Western Civilization is certainly not the only one in the world, it is the most dominant one on this planet in terms of economic and military prowess. Let's examine our current Western Civilization.

> *Only about 13.1% of the world population is Western; however we provide nearly 50% of the world's gross economic product and occupy 24% of the world's territory. Huntington argues with strong reason that Western Civilization peaked in about 1920 and has been in considerable decline since that time. In 1920, 48% of the world population was Western and the West provided nearly 85% of the world's manufacturing output. By these measures, we are not as dominant as we once were.*

Only one major world power was left standing at the end of the Cold War - the United States, leader of Western Civilization. This led to a feeling of euphoria in the U.S. that Western Civilization had won the world and its principles would prevail around the world. We are now awakening to a different reality. The alliances in the world during the Cold War were between two military superpowers who dominated the species; the Western system survived and the communist one did not (except for remnants). Since the Cold War ended, conflict and tension have now developed along civilization differences.

The West has viewed itself as the center of the world and has largely assumed that its civilization will become the de facto world civilization. It has been easy for people in the U.S. to perceive the world in this manner. It has been more than 200 years since we have had foreign conflict on our soil. Most people in the US have not traveled abroad. Compared to others in the world, most of us have a comfortable standard of living and are very consumed by our many earthly pleasures. It has been easy for us to be lulled into a sense that the world is ours. This is not unlike the conditions in Rome before the fall.

For most Americans it is easy to get caught up in our daily provincial lives because we exist in isolation from the rest of the world. We view ourselves as the premiere human civilization and seem to think this should be unquestioned by others. We certainly are not the only civilization on the planet, and it remains to be determined if we are the best. Throughout the history of humans, many civilizations have risen and have also fallen.

Our euphoria ended on 9/11/2001. In our lifetime memories, up until the events of that day, we largely felt that we had won the world and that it was ours to guide. On that day we became aware of the clash of civilizations on our planet.

Tensions in the world today are not between nations - they are between civilizations.

Conflict

The West is currently in competition and conflict with the Islamic Civilization and, to a lesser extent, with the Sinic (Chinese) Civilization. The conflict is mostly without blood, but it seems to clearly manifest in group relations.

Both Islam and China have long-standing cultural traditions that are very different from the West and, in their judgment, are superior. Both Christianity and Islam teach that their god is universal and is the god for everyone, and they are both taught to be missionary about their beliefs. This creates a fundamental conflict with one another.

Other civilizations on this planet do not accept the West as the eventual leader of all humans. Quite the contrary, they seem to totally oppose our leadership. They believe they have many good reasons to oppose us. They believe that their civilizations are better than or at least equal to ours. We need to examine their points of view. We must also be open-minded and consider that they may be right on some matters.

Why I wouldn't like us if I was on the outside

I am a product of Western Civilization, and hence, probably cannot be objective about this topic. However, being from the West gives me greater insight about its organization and also more license to be self-critical. I apologize in advance if my self-evaluation of Western Civilization offends.

I would see us as being imperialistic. We impose the structure of our civilization on others. Just as we believe our Judeo-Christian God is their God (we believe that they simply have not yet accepted that fact), we also assume that our civilization structure is best for everyone else and should be so embraced.

I would see us as aggressive. Look at the history of Western aggression against other Civilizations and cultures. We can begin with the crusades in the 11th and 12th centuries in which Western Christians repeatedly marched to the Middle East and killed Muslims. Western imperialism was the clear pattern in the world during the 16th to 19th centuries as imperialistic Spanish, British, Dutch and French navies carved up the world. During the 20th century the U.S. was militarily imperialistic towards Latin America and the Philippines. The history of the 20th century was dominated by two world wars - both of which were largely among nations of the Western Civilization. In more recent times the U.S., in particular, has shown imperialistic aggression in Korea, Vietnam, Iraq, Afghanistan, and Iraq again. Throughout recent history, the West has had supremacy in military technology. The U.S. is also the only country to have used nuclear weaponry in a war - a fact not lost on others. And now the U.S. has such sophisticated weapons that we can conduct push-button wars and watch them on television.

I would also see us as a decadent society that is based upon greed and without moral convictions. Ours is a capitalistic system in which individuals are motivated by self-desires and not according to group-responsibility. Others do not see the facts that capitalism is designed to meet the common good. Our system motivates people according to their self-serving needs. It would be easy to see selfishness without concern for others. It would also be easy to see wanton waste and materialism that is especially bothersome given their relative poverty and growing scarcity of the planet's resources. The benefits of capitalism to the group, although they are very powerful, are not easily apparent to an outsider.

I would also see a civilization with many human problems: crime, murder, full prisons, poverty within our inner cities, drugs, moral decay, moral depravity, sexual promiscuity, and full mental institutions. They do not have those problems nearly to the same extent.

I would see us as two-faced. One of the major foundations of our country, expressed in our Declaration of Independence proclaims that "All men are created equal". However, this did not stop us from treating Native American Indians as less-than-equal, nor from ignoring the rights of Mexican settlers in gold country in California despite treaties stating otherwise, nor from enslaving millions of African Americans, nor from withholding rights from women. More recently we invaded Iraq on the basis of weapons of mass destruction; then ignored the fact that they were never found.

THE WESTERN DIFFERENCES AS VIEWED BY OTHERS

In Western Civilization we emphasize the individual. Our Declaration of Independence says, "We hold these truths to be self-evident, that all men are created equal, that they are endowed by their Creator with certain unalienable rights, and that among these are Life, Liberty and the pursuit of Happiness". Huntington states that the greatest distinguishing characteristic between Western Civilization and others is the large role and emphasis of the individual. Our system emphasizes the individual and the rights of the individual.

Just as capitalism drives individual humans based upon their self-serving needs, capitalism has also driven Western Civilization to meet its self-serving needs. The 17 countries with the highest gross domestic product per person are all Western - with the possible exception of Japan - although Japan acts similar to a Western country. Of all the world millionaires, 60% are in North America or Europe. Clearly the West has the greatest monetary wealth on the planet.

Now, imagine that you are on the outside looking in at this situation. Imagine that you are a religious fundamentalist who believes that people should be motivated by the religious values of group responsibility and by the nobler principles of morality and ethics. Would you be critical of the system driven by self-desire? Would you judge the other system as selfish? Of course you would! Would you feel even more strongly if your own self-desires were satisfied less because of the greed and competitiveness of the other system? Would you feel even more strongly if the other system were militarily strong and aggressive?

Of course, we (Western Civilization) are that other system. The followers of Islam believe in a religion-driven state that teaches and motivates largely through religious values. I think the reasons they do not like us are clear. The reasons they do not like us are also driven by righteousness. They can claim the high road when it comes to motivating people.

In the United States we have been strongly influenced by the free speech and individual rights movements of the 1960's. Doctor Benjamin Spock, known as "the father of permissiveness", had strong influence on individual liberalism by suggesting that children should be encouraged to do as they want with reduced discipline. The 1980's became the "Me Generation". "If you've got it, flaunt it" and "You can have it all!" became generational mantras. Binge buying, "Shop 'til you Drop", and credit card debts have now become a way of life.

Followers of Islam, on the other hand, put religion first in their life. They consider themselves to be God-fearing people who live a life of and with God. Their religious laws even supersede those of government. They believe they take the high road (i.e., "nobler road") in life and believe they live quality lives. They want to continue to live their lives the way they desire without us infringing upon them. However, our civilization pervades theirs. Whether it is MacDonald's hamburgers, Madonna, or Star Wars movies, Western culture invades other cultures. We are invasive upon their civilization militarily, economically and culturally.

The West has largely won the world because of our stranglehold on the resources of this planet and because of our military superiority and aggression. It is easy for others to perceive us as an evil empire that is taking over the world with selfishness and bullying tactics. It is not surprising that some others resort to desperate tactics to oppose us. We should view terrorism as acts of desperation rather than acts of zealots.

Western Civilization has led to amazing developments in science, technology and human comforts. However, it has been at the expense of aggression towards other civilizations and greed that has resulted in tremendous imbalance in resource ownership.

The United States is obviously the most powerful economic and military nation in the world. We are clearly the leader of Western Civilization, but we are also clearly NOT the leader of all world civilizations. Will Western Civilization be able to lead the human race to its future?

Can Western Civilization Strength Continue?

Homo sapiens are at the top of the life pyramid on this planet and are organized into civilizations that represent the main groupings of our species. Western Civilization can claim to have been the strongest species group during the 20th century.

Homo sapiens live in a Darwinian world, and survival of the fittest still is the rule. Is Western Civilization suited to lead our species into the Darwinian future?

Summary - Right and Left Brain balance in Civilizations

The depths of ·life and Darwinian survival come to us from our feeling right brain. The vision-based neurology of our "silent" right brain has been the primary Darwinian survival mechanism of nearly all vertebrate life forms (including humans) since the Cambrian Life Explosion.

The story of our species and its' civilizations has been that of the development of our unique speech-based and thinking left brain and how it has interacted with the already-existing right brain.

Our left brain enabled us to separate ourselves from the animals, and then enabled us to dominate all other life forms on the planet and to aggressively develop the planet's resources to meet our needs and desires. Our strong grouping instincts, which fundamentally come from the depths of Darwinian survival since the Cambrian era, have been supported and nurtured by our left-brain group think. Current and past Civilizations use different strategies of incorporating left and right.

The accomplishments of our thinking left brain in species development are immense and they have played a major role in defining the current existence status of our species. However, what should be the role of the right brain in our current guidance and the future of our species? Is participation by the Darwinian right side needed? Or, is the right-brain guidance vestigial? Has it been superseded by the left brain? The grouping strategies of major Civilizations are quite different from one another. In particular, the differences between East and West include a large difference in orientation towards the right and left brains respectively.

Human history suggests that we need to incorporate the right brain in our group governance. The argument here is that the seeds for destruction of the Greco-Roman Empire, the first real left brain civilization, were sown when democracy, it's only real inclusion of the right brain, was eliminated by Julius Caesar. Western Civilization emerged from the ashes of the Dark Ages both with a god and with democracy restored. This suggests that we need to include the right brain in our group organization.

To the extent that the right brain must be involved in our future, Eastern and Islamic Civilizations currently operate with a greater participation of the right brain in their Civilizations than does the West. This seems advantageous if survival of Homo sapiens becomes more challenged: such as would occur with overpopulation with finite resources.

If our species encounters over-population with limited resources, Eastern and Islamic Civilizations are much better positioned for survival because of their stronger attachment to the right brain sense of group. Eastern and Islamic Civilizations already support larger populations of people with considerably fewer consumable items and lower GDP/person. I don't believe the West would be able to do likewise unless the transition to reduced resources is slow and stable to enable it to adapt. If our species becomes challenged by famine or subservience to another species, I predict that Islamic and Eastern Civilizations would survive much better than Western.

Triumvirate Analysis

The success of Western Civilization at leading the future of our species will depend, at least in part, upon the extent to which the triumvirate of science, capitalism and democracy, with a dash of religion, can meet the Darwinian Life Drive that comes from our right brain.

Is there an inner voice that needs to be better represented in our civilization in order to more truly meet the Life Drive? Has the left brain developed to the point that it has outgrown the need to include the right brain in guiding our civilization? Should formal religion play a larger role – or is the current role of "conscience" the correct one? These are difficult questions to answer.

Science has no direction or real guidance from the right brain. However, as the arbiter of truth in our society, the outcomes of science often act in the role of the judiciary to answer factual questions in guiding our civilization. It is difficult to find fault with or recommend altering science as a mainstay of Western Civilization. The application of scientific principles to the study of nature seems to clearly serve the collective good by providing us with valid answers and information about the world around us.

The role of science in Western Civilization is one of its greatest strengths; this role is probably ideal and should not be changed. However, science could help us better design our future by studying the human core, human motivation, and the optimal social methods of organizing humans for group success. In other words, science should study god and religion. This may help to answer some of the difficult questions regarding the optimal roles of the left and right brain functions in guiding our future.

Democracy, by its very nature, allows all individuals to participate in making group decisions. Democracy allows all people to participate in governance decisions and to cast their votes based upon the feelings of their right brain and/or upon the thoughts of their left brain. Democracy seems well-designed to combine the inputs from our right-brain Life Drive and from our Human left-brain.

As apparently demonstrated by the fall of the Roman Empire, democracy is a necessary component of a civilization led by left-brain reasoning.

Capitalism is an immensely successful system that enables the West to harness the planet's resources for our success. It actually creates Darwinian struggle and competition for our left brain. Capitalism definitely operates with "survival of the fittest" as part of its modus operandi.

Capitalism is a very strong part of the foundation for Western Civilization, and it seems certain that it will remain so.

Is the Triumvirate Working?

Western Civilization's triumvirate (capitalism, democracy, and science) has been very successful at meeting the needs of individuals and also enabling group success. It has resulted in greater human comfort for its members and greater ability to influence (and *dominate*) other Homo sapiens civilizations. By these measures, the West has attained Homo sapiens pre-eminence. The West stumbled before with the Roman demise into the

Dark Ages, it is possible that any shortcoming or weakness in the current system may eventually lead to its demise again.

One area in which the triumvirate may be deficient is that nothing in the system directly motivates people according to their group needs or responsibilities. John F. Kennedy hit the nail on the head when he said: "Ask not what your country can do for you: Ask what you can do for your country". In our system there are too many individuals who are only motivated to get what they want for themselves, and they do not take responsibility for their own behavior or contributions towards the group.

> *The Bill of Rights is a prominent part of the U.S. constitution. This specifies individual rights and sets up the individualism in our country. However, rights should not come without responsibilities. Perhaps we should also have a Bill of Responsibilities, because it is critical that individuals contribute to the group.*

Huntington points to the following conditions as leading to the current decline of Western Civilization:

- Increases in anti-social behavior such as crime, drug use and violence.
- Family decay as evidenced by divorce, illegitimacy, dead-beat parents, etc.
- Decreased participation in social organizations with altruistic missions
- Weakening of the work ethic
- Decreased commitment to learning and intellectual activity

We must consider that the above conditions result from lack of concern for individual contributions to the whole - i.e. lack of motivation according to group-responsibility. Others would say that these conditions result from too-little emphasis on religion. It is very possible that too many people today are out to get what is good for themselves, and have too little concern for contributions to others or the group – or to the morals taught by religion. This is related to the strong emphasis on individualism in Western Civilization. This emphasis on meeting self-needs does not exist in other civilizations in the world. Others have a greater emphasis on moral responsibilities for contribution to the group.

Possibly the largest weakness of our triumvirate is failure to adequately motivate individuals according to the needs of the group.

Individuals within our system, of course, have complete freedom to pursue the pleasures of meeting their group-responsibility needs, but it may be that this passive motivation of group-responsibility needs is not enough. Sometimes it seems that too many people are not adequately internally stimulated to meet their group-responsibility needs - apparently the lure of meeting self-desires is too strong.

Religion and Science Relationship

Religion and science should work hand in hand with one another. It is usually detrimental to any Civilization when they oppose one another.

Current religious teachings in the West are based upon dogma. The Judeo-Christian religions have remained largely fixed in their beliefs for 2000-2500 years. During that time, science has made immense discoveries about nature - and much about the origins of humans. Religious leaders have rejected many of the findings of science because they conflict with the older religious teachings. This places religion in direct opposition to science and that which is otherwise accepted as truth in our civilization.

Religion has not grown with our civilization and, because of its strict adherence to dogma and non-acceptance of scientific findings, has tarnished its own credibility. In so doing, religion has compromised its own contribution towards meeting group and individual needs in the West. This has led to an under-representation of the altruistic human needs to contribute to the group.

Western Civilization would likely be strengthened by a religion that used and worked with science. There should be no fundamental or inherent conflict between science and religion. If there is a god, there can only be one god that represents the truth about life. Religion and science can jointly orient towards that ultimate truth.

Religion should be aware of the past, but also be willing to grow and accept what we learn about ourselves and the world around us. We also would benefit if science dedicated itself to understanding human nature and human motivation, and also accept that there may be an ultimate unknown. Religion should accept the findings of science, and use them to refine religious beliefs and teachings. The core of religion should be the essence of Life itself. That is where god is.

God and Religion in the West

The West, dominated by its left brain and its higher reliance on ego satisfaction, emerged from the Dark Ages with the Judeo-Christian God. How does religion currently fit into Western Civilization organization?

In the West, God and religion are not a fundamental institution in the same way as the triumvirate of science, capitalism, and democracy. God is more like a conscience to be applied as needed, as shown in Figure 24. Religion does not have a formalized role in Western societies; in fact, the first amendment to the U.S. Constitution formalizes the separation of church and state and explicitly forbids the participation of church in state. "Congress shall make no law respecting an establishment of religion, or prohibiting the free exercise thereof..." first amendment, U.S. Constitution.

Democracy is an institution with a recognized and defined purpose in Western Civilization. Religion is specifically barred from such a role. Therefore religion has no official power, only the power to influence and participate as people choose to allow it.

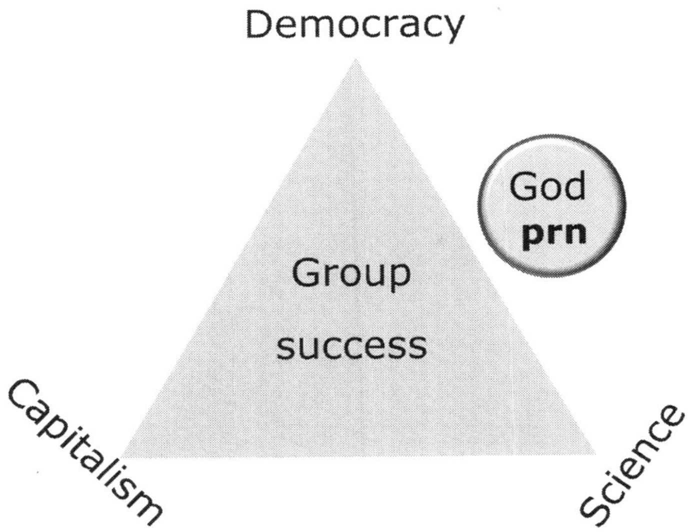

Figure 24. *God and religion are not a formal part of the triumvirate that serves as the foundation for the West. Instead, God and religion are like a conscience and can exert influence on any of the three triumvirate institutions. God can be used as needed ("prn" is medical term for "as needed").*

The religious teachings of the Christian God, consistent with similar teachings in other civilizations, eschew the worldly pleasures. This form of human motivation is different than capitalism which motivates people by satisfying self-desires. Religion can add a sense of fairness and ethics that may influence capitalistic behavior. Religion is definitely not part of democracy, as stated in the U.S. Constitution. However, religion can play a large influential role in democracy as demonstrated by the strong Christian coalition organized by Karl Rove and George Bush, Jr. Likewise, religion does not have a direct role in science, but it can exert influence over science as demonstrated by ongoing controversies about cloning, abortion, and stem cell research.

Religion can be influential on each of the triumvirate institutions: capitalism, democracy, and science.

Religion can also just as readily be ignored when it gets in the way of group success. Christian teachings could never support the actions of the first Europeans towards the Incans, the 17th-20th Century Imperialist actions of the West, the actions of the U.S. to Native Americans, the actions of the U.S. towards Mexican settlers on the gold fields of California, or most of the military actions of the U.S. since WW2. Religion is applied as needed (prn) to meet group success.

God and religion in the West are applied as needed (prn) and ignored when they obstruct group desires or success. This often results in duplicitous behavior.

The Western tie to the God of Abraham is weak compared to Islam. In Islam, God is much more central to the Civilization's structure.

SUMMARY

The West has been hugely successful because the human left brain has been given the largest leadership and governance role. The ties to group responsibility and to the right brain are relatively weak compared to Islam and to the East. Democracy is the formal Western tie with the right brain, God and religion also play a less formal but influential tie with the right brain and the group.

The West emerged from the ashes of the Dark Ages with a God to be applied as needed. Western Civilization now has an added tie to the survivalist right brain and to our sense of group. The fall of the Roman Empire appears to demonstrate that democracy is necessary. The left brain, with the initial actions and influence of Julius Caesar, eliminated democracy which led to the eventual demise of the hugely successful Roman Empire. Democracy is needed for continued success and we are right to cling to it. However, democracy was lost previously and it could happen again.

Religion currently plays a large influential role on democracy, and also has influences on science and capitalism. Religion serves to further ground Western Civilization in the right brain and the sense of group. In addition to the effects of democracy, the influence of religion appears to help prevent a future disintegration such as occurred in the Dark Ages.

Civilizations and *Homo sapiens* Future

Currently there are several competing civilizations on our planet, and the signs of conflict between them are clear and growing. Will we eventually have a single civilization? Or will we continue to have several? Which is best for our species?

Group success is ultimately most important for survival of our species. There have been numerous different governance systems throughout our history and throughout our current world. There is current Darwinian competition among civilizations for influence over our planet's resources, its people, and ultimately the future of the species. Accordingly the most successful civilizations or governance systems are the ones that we see today. Previous civilizations and governance structures, such as the earliest civilizations, have passed into history because they could not compete and survive with newer civilizations that evolved.

We are clearly reliant upon one another and the ultimate success and happiness of each individual depends upon success of the group. A governance system that is attuned to and harnesses the individual and collective human mind will likely also be most successful at nurturing human potential and at leading *Homo sapiens* into the future. It is likely that the most successful group in the long run will be the one in which individual satisfaction and group success work in harmony.

At first thought, it seems that humans on this planet will be best served if we live cooperatively and in harmony - something probably best accomplished if we all were within the same civilization. However, it is also possible that, just as monopolies are not good for the development of commerce and business, civilization monopoly may not be good for our future.

It also seems highly unlikely that, given history and the current status, humans can all agree on a single civilization. Possibly the only scenario in which the human species would cooperate worldwide, and work within a single civilization, would be in response to a common and external threat such as from an extra-terrestrial source.

Perhaps Darwinian struggle and competition among civilizations is what is best for our future? – just as healthy competition is necessary for growth within a capitalistic system. This line of thought advocates for continuance of multiple civilizations with competition and struggle between them, as peacefully as possible, for influence over resources, people, and our species.

RIGHT AND LEFT ROLES IN HOMO SAPIENS FUTURE

For our future it is almost certainly best that we think of left and right brains as partners in guiding our species. Frankly, our future would look bleak without either the left or the right brain cognitive leadership. Also, I suspect that if the right and left brains cannot get along with one another, we are doomed to go through future cycles such as the Dark Ages and Renaissance.

> *St Augustine, author of City of God, correctly identified the differences between the City of God and the City of Man. The will of god is located in our right brain, and the will of humans (man) in our left. The left brain is skilled at building our civilization; the right brain contains secrets of Life and has played the major role in insuring our species' evolutionary survival and development. The essence of Life, whatever "Life" is, comes to us through our right brain. (The next chapter speculates on the nature of "Life".)*

The left-brain reasoning of man seems unable to run our civilization, by itself, without offending the right brain. This is a lesson we should have learned when the left brain of Rome ran out of control and the right brain came back to put us in our place. Too much human control leads to too much greed and selfishness. On the other hand, too much control by the right brain results in lack of ambition, drive, and civilization progress.

Following the Life Truth emanating from our right brain seems good at enabling humans to work together within the group and at spreading the available resources rather evenly across a population. This was necessary when we were hunter/gatherers and when we evolved into larger city groups and even into the early civilizations. This is also the way in which human beings can live most harmoniously with nature. Each person takes no more than they need and each also feels duty and obligation to contribute to the group. This is also why religious strategy worked so well during the Dark Ages, when the infra-structure of Western Civilization collapsed with the fall of the Roman Empire. Humans learned to and needed to survive with little.

To the extent that humans are constrained by a limited environmental space and with limited resources, the right-brain survivalist leadership likely will best serve our species. Thomas Malthus (1766-1834) observed that, in nature, plants and animals produce far more offspring than can survive, and that humans too are capable of overproducing if left unchecked. Malthus concluded that unless family size was regulated, famine would become globally epidemic and eventually consume humans. Malthus' view that poverty and famine were natural outcomes of population growth and food supply was not popular among social reformers who believed that with proper social structures, all ills of man could be eradicated. Pure right-brain leadership in this situation would manage the situation in the natural and instinctual manner – just as it would be managed in animal groups. The right brain is a much better survivor than the left brain.

Malthus' prediction has come partially true. There are many regions of the world today in which poverty and starvation are rampant. The areas of the world living in poverty are generally the same ones that have right brain- and group-leaning civilizations. Is it because religion leads to that conclusion, or is it because religion is the best manner in which to cope with those conditions? It may not even matter which caused which, because they seem to naturally gravitate to one another.

Malthus did not envision the immense success of capitalism and science at harvesting the planet's resources to meet human needs within Western Civilization. Because of this immense success that has occurred since Malthus' time, misery and famine are not as rampant as might have been predicted – especially in Western Civilization. This human-lead civilization is generating such a wealth of resources that consumerism and wealth accumulation are much more common than poverty. This is the work of the left brain. The left brain is capable of increasing the utility of the resources around us.

Right now the left brain is dominant in guiding Western Civilization. For us to lead our species into the future we must use the reasoning strengths in the left brain, but also listen to the right brain and keep it satisfied. Our species loses its orientation towards Life when the left brain is the only one steering.

THE WESTERN ROLE IN HOMO SAPIENS FUTURE

Does the current situation of hunger in the world, global warming, finite and apparently limited food production, and limited oil and mineral resources lead us to conclude that we are headed towards a Malthusian condition? ...best managed by the right brain... Or, can left brain-developed human technologies such as those of silicon chips, communications, travel, biotechnology, harvesting asteroid minerals, and the numerous other advancements of our Western Civilization avoid such an ending and offer us a land of plenty?

Western Civilization is largely about a greater role of the human left brain. Anyone who believes in Western Civilization as the future leader almost necessarily must also believe that left brain leadership is the better strategy for our collective future. (Please note the use of the word *believe.*)

There is a caveat....we *must* listen to the right brain. The right brain *is* who we are at our core. We should endeavor to understand our right brain core as completely as possible – even though the very depths of the core will likely be inaccessible to human investigation. A marriage of theology, including all religions, with science could work in this direction. This could finally lead us to the realization that there is only one ultimate truth (god) in Life.

History seems to have proven that democracy is a necessary companion to a left-brain-led civilization. Democracy, probably in its purest form, is that for which we must strive.....worldwide. Since the Renaissance, Western Civilization has made great strides at improving the implementation of democracy. The monarchies of Europe have been replaced.

The imperialism and colonialism of the 18th and nineteenth centuries have ended and most acquired countries have now been given their freedom. Slavery has been abolished. Women, blacks, and other minorities have been given rights. We have made significant strides to decrease unfair discrimination. Democracy has also recently experienced much greater influence and acceptance in countries previously under dictatorial control.

We are not perfect, but the trends since the Renaissance all seem to be moving in the correct direction. Worse than our own errors of implementation has been our lack of involving the non-Western world in the future of humans.

> *The left brain is out of the bag and cannot be put back in. It needs to understand its partner in life, the right brain, so that they can dance together into our future.*

CHAPTER 10

WHAT IS LIFE?

The investigation contained in this book has pondered Life. So, what is Life? First, a definition:

"Life" is the life we observe on this planet, and also likely that which we seek to find elsewhere in our solar system or the universe. "LIFE" is the unknown entity towards which Life strives, thereby causing Darwinian competition and survival.

Next, a bit of summary:

All forms of Life, including Homo sapiens, participate in an unrelenting pursuit of LIFE that propels each species into the Darwinian struggle for survival. From what we know, this seems to have been the situation ever since the beginning of Life on this planet. Pursuit of LIFE drives this Darwinian struggle.

Our individual and collective human consciousness comes from the cognitive abilities based upon the neural wiring for vision (right brain) and speech (left brain). We think with our left brain, but LIFE comes to us from our right brain.

LIFE has been central to the entire history of life on this planet – from first single cell organism up through the Civilization structure of Homo sapiens. The emergence of humans with left-brain thinking has not altered this scenario.

LIFE remains central to just about everything in the affairs of the species that labels itself "Homo sapiens". No other species are predatory to Homo sapiens. Homo sapiens can concentrate on improving its comfort and strength. It is the left brain that separated Homo sapiens from other forms of Life, and it is the left brain that enabled it to be in its current situation. The left brain was created by Life as it pursued LIFE.

Each of the major species groups, called "Civilizations", honors LIFE as part of their group mind. One of the recent Civilizations (called "Western") actually attempted to forget that LIFE is central and must be part of the Civilization structure. It quickly failed and needed a God in order to continue as a group.

So, there IS something called LIFE and it appears to have a singular definition.... but, what is it?

This chapter summarizes what our journey has taught us about LIFE, and what we can do about it. It begins with speculation that LIFE is a major component of the universe and that it is configured with the Einsteinian parameters of time, space, gravity, and speed. It concludes with analysis of what LIFE means to our species and to each of us.

LIFE and the Universe

> *LIFE has an immense effect upon all Life as we know it, all Life pursues it. It is possible that LIFE can be recognized in 2 "locations" – deep inside each individual and somewhere in the Universe. We should consider the possibility that LIFE is in both locations.*

> *This section proposes how LIFE may be configured in the universe.*

The discovery of amino acids in meteorites (Murchison meteorite) strongly suggests that Life came to this planet from elsewhere. Also, in combination with the immensity of the Universe, it seems most reasonable to conclude that Life exists elsewhere in the Universe. The assumption here is that LIFE is a universal concept. Therefore, life elsewhere in the universe, like life on this planet, is engaged in pursuit of LIFE.

The Big Bang and Theory of Relativity

If LIFE is somewhere in the universe, then we should investigate what we know about the universe and attempt to identify LIFE. We begin by investigating what we know about the Big Bang and the Theory of Relativity.

Until the 20th century, our observations and scientific study led us to understand that the heavens we observe from our planet extended infinitely in all directions. Edwin Hubble, however, determined that the universe is expanding, galaxies of stars are moving away from one another, and the velocity of each galaxy is proportional to its distance. Galaxies that are twice as far from us move twice as fast. The galaxies are moving as if they all originated from one spot.

Hubble's discoveries served as the basis for the Big Bang Theory, which is the dominant theory about the origin of the universe among physicists and astronomers. According to this theory a large explosion created the universe more than 13 billion years ago. Prior to the explosion, apparently all the matter in the universe existed in one spot. Gravity was infinite. We have difficulty conceptualizing that all the matter in the universe was at one time concentrated in one spot, but such difficulty results from the fact that our entire experiences are based upon the conditions we experience at our particular location and condition in the universe. We adapt well to the situations we encounter, but have difficulty relating to those we have not encountered.

Albert Einstein's Theory of Relativity leads to similar difficult-to-relate-to conclusions. The scientific community accepts the Theory of Relativity and observable facts support it. This theory states that there are certain fundamental relations between time, gravity, space, and mass. The relationships among these entities depend upon the speed of movement through the universe. The speed of light is considered to be the speed limit of the observable universe.

The Theory of Relativity states that as speed of movement in the universe increases:

- time slows
- gravity increases
    - mass increases
    - size decreases

The above configuration suggests that the 2 primary entities that are affected by speed of movement are time and gravity. Mass and size are shown as being secondary to changes in gravity. This is because, as gravity increases, size will become smaller and mass will become greater (denser). Although these changes all occur together, the changes in time and gravity seem most fundamental and the changes in size and mass seem secondary to the changes in gravity.

As the speed of light (186,000 miles/second) is approached, time comes near to a full stop and gravity becomes immense. As result, mass increases towards infinity, and size approaches zero.

At the speed of light these all become absolutes.

- time stops ("no time")
- gravity becomes infinite
    - mass becomes infinite
    - size becomes infinitesimal

We have difficulty conceptualizing "no time" and "infinite gravity". Our entire existence and all of our life experiences are within the small range of time and speed conditions that exist for us on our planet. The velocity range that any of us normally experiences is contained within a very, very small range. The greatest speed difference most of us experience is about 600 miles/hour – the relative speed we attain in an aircraft. This is minuscule compared to the speed of light, which is approximately 67,000,000 miles/hour. We do not have any real life experience with the conditions that exist at speeds close to the speed of light; they are totally outside of our human experience and we cannot relate to them. However, these conditions *do* exist elsewhere in the universe.

Reconciling Big Bang and the Theory of Relativity

By reconciling these 2 theories, we can derive information that helps in our quest to define LIFE.

The Big Bang Theory tells us that before "the bang" all the mass of the universe was contained in an extremely small spot (infinitesimal). This means gravity was infinite. If gravity was infinite, then time was likely stopped and the infinitesimal point with infinite mass was travelling at the speed of light.

The conditions prior to the Big Bang seem to be exactly what Einstein's theory predicts if an object is moving at the speed of light. Gravity was infinite resulting in infinite mass and infinitesimal size. Time also must have been slowed to a stop. If time was stopped prior to the bang, we are led to conclude that time in our universe literally began with the Big Bang.

Prior to the Big Bang, infinite mass in an infinitesimally small point (gravity was infinite) was traveling at the speed of light and time was stopped. Time literally began with the Big Bang.

Another thing to consider is the existence of black holes in the universe. Black holes are known to have immense gravitational pull; the gravity is so strong that even light cannot escape, and this is why they appear black. All matter in the area of a black hole (stars and galaxies) seems to be drawn into the hole. We should consider that the conditions within the black hole are the same as those that existed prior to the Big Bang. It is as if portions of our current observable universe are being subjected to infinite gravity and mass, small size, and traveling at the speed of light.... into black holes. Perhaps black holes are portals to other universes?

These are the conditions that occur at the speed of light, they also are the conditions that existed just prior to the Big Bang and also in Black Holes:

- Time = 0
- Gravity = ∞

  - Mass = ∞
  - Size = 0
- Speed = c (speed of light)

The Big Bang was the beginning of time as we know it. Is time infinite? It is quite easy to grasp the concept of an infinite future. However, it seems not possible to comfortably grasp the concept of an infinite past. It is much easier to grasp the concept of a beginning point in time. The Big Bang Theory matches with our inner ability to conceptualize time.

WHAT CAUSED THE BIG BANG?

Answering this question inevitably leads to the first cause theory postulated by Saint Thomas Aquinas. If an event happens, something must have triggered it. If some event happens, something must have existed prior to the event in order to cause it to happen. Theoretically, there can't be an uncaused first cause. If all of the matter was concentrated in one small spot, what caused it to slow down from the speed of light and explode? There must have been a cause behind the Big Bang. The Big Bang did not just happen - something had to cause it. As with every unknown, god can be placed at the end of the line of reasoning. Is it possible that the pursuit of LIFE (and god) is what caused the Big Bang?

LIFE AS THE ANTI-BIG BANG

Consider the following possibilities:

LIFE played a role in causing the Big Bang.
LIFE is the condition towards which the post-Big Bang universe moves.
LIFE is the condition opposite to the Before Big Bang condition

As developed above, at the moment Before the Big Bang (BBB), all the matter in our observable universe was contained in a very small size travelling at the speed of light. Time was zero and gravity was infinite. This set of conditions is shown in the Before Big Bang (BBB) column in Table 2. After the Big Bang (ABB) each of these primary entities moved towards its opposite condition (Anti-BB) as noted in the Table. Anti-BB is the condition opposite the Big Bang and is proposed as the LIFE condition.

Table2. *Conditions Before and After the Big Bang (BBB and ABB). The final column shows the the Anti-Big Bang, or LIFE, condition.*

	BBB	ABB	Anti-BB "Life"?
Size	0	Towards ∞	∞
Gravity	∞	Towards 0	0
Mass	∞	Towards 0	0
Time	0	Towards ∞, but finite	∞
Speed	∞	Towards 0, but finite	0

It seems reasonable to hypothesize that Life is the Anti-BB condition – the opposite of the condition just prior to the Big Bang. Matter and energy (which are basically the same or inter-changeable) are pawn material that gravity and space/time manipulate as their conditions vacillate between the poles (BBB and Anti-BB).

As gravity swings from infinite (BBB) to zero (Anti-BB), matter and energy likewise vacillate between the BBB condition in which matter and energy are in a single spot (e.g. black holes) and the Anti-BB condition where they are everywhere (e.g. the edge of the universe). Gravity and time seem in an endless dance in which they move oppositely – each being zero when the other is infinite. Our Earth and solar system exists at a midway point where both gravity and time have finite values; the observable universe likewise exists at midway points. We seem unable to directly observe either end point (BBB or Anti-BB); we seem unable to see into a black hole or to the edge of the universe.

Gravity and time each becomes zero when the other is infinite. Attaining either infinity or zero, which occurs at the BBB and Anti-BB end conditions, seems untenable for either gravity or time. As result the universe, as we are able to observe it, exists between these two end conditions. Gravity is infinite at one end condition (BBB and black holes); time is infinite at the other end condition (edge of universe, Anti-BB). Neither end condition seems sustainable because of the seemingly impossibilities of "zero" and "infinity". Each end condition is unstable.

The universe exists between 2 end conditions: infinite gravity (BBB) and infinite time (Anti-BB). LIFE can be considered to be the Anti-BB condition.

If LIFE is the Anti-BB condition, then the BBB condition, in which gravity is infinite, can be considered the anti-LIFE condition.

If LIFE is the Anti-BB condition, then LIFE is infinite time and zero gravity. Infinite time, in which time becomes infinitely fast, is difficult to conceptualize. The interpretation here is that infinite time is the same as time being "forever". Zero gravity means that there is no hold on matter and energy; hence matter and energy exist in an infinite space that is everywhere. Therefore, the LIFE condition, which is the same as the Anti-BB condition, is everywhere and forever.

LIFE is everywhere and forever.

Life as we know it pursues something called LIFE. This is what drives Darwinian survival and evolution. As developed earlier, all Life on this planet is in pursuit of something called "LIFE". This also applies to our human civilizations which, on a larger scale, can be said to likewise be engaged in Darwinian struggle and organized to pursue LIFE. Our civilizations are oriented towards LIFE by their adherence to belief in God or to universal truths such as harmony and enlightenment. "Everywhere" and "forever" are characteristics assigned to God (in the Bible) and also to the truths about life espoused in Eastern Civilizations rooted in the teachings of Buddha and Confucius.

The theory here is that LIFE is the Anti-BB condition, where gravity is zero and time is infinite. If true, then LIFE is everywhere and forever. These concepts are compatible with Western, Islamic, and Eastern teachings.

LIFE AND LIFE

In the collective and individual human mind, LIFE comes to us from our vision-based right brain. Of course, LIFE goes much deeper into life history than our right brain, but the closest touch our mind has with LIFE comes to us from our vision-based right mind. Vision has led Darwinian survival on this planet for 570 million years. Pursuit of LIFE has been the objective and it drives survival.

We can treat LIFE as an unknown black box and use it as a beacon to guide us. At first, that might seem like a strange metaphor: a black box beacon. But, that seems true. We are led by, attracted to, and driven by a strong central beacon that is also a huge unknown black box. We really don't know what it is, but it seems big. It is LIFE.

Try to imagine how awe-struck our earliest ancestors were by the power, harmony, beauty, size, and wonders of the world that surrounded them, and in which they were inescapably immersed. We have been in awe of our surroundings from the beginning. There was a strong awareness of LIFE in the vision-based animal world from which we came, and our fledgling left brain consciousness was in awe of it. We are still in awe of LIFE - when we allow ourselves to really experience it.

Early in our history, God became the symbol and representative of the ultimate force of Life. This seems a fact and matters not whether you adhere to a belief about god. God is a great epicenter to honor, represent, and organize species groups towards LIFE. Belief in God is actually belief in LIFE.

The Islamic civilization strongly places God at the center of their Civilization; that is how Islam anchors its center in LIFE. The West also honors and respects God, but not as the centerpiece. Instead, the West has a triumvirate of institutions. The triumvirate is heavily weighted to the left brain. Only democracy has an element of the right brain. History seems to have taught us that the West likely needs both democracy and God (even if only "as needed") for its continuance. The West continually struggles with what appears to be a conflict between God (LIFE) and science (left brain deduction). The Islamic and Western groups of *Homo sapiens* both honor LIFE through a god.

The Eastern groups of Homo sapiens civilizations honor LIFE by placing Tao, enlightenment, or harmony at the center of their civilizations.

All major human groups seem to have a strong orientation to LIFE. They should, because LIFE is that to which our species strives.

Homo sapiens have honored LIFE from the very beginning of its existence. The major groups of *Homo sapiens* each have a central orientation towards LIFE, just as human groups have done throughout history.

Life, as we know it, is governed by Darwinian struggle to survive. Darwinian "survival of the fittest" is the strategy that Life uses to survive and succeed. The pursuit of LIFE is central to the Darwinian drive to survive. The pursuit of LIFE seems central to all.

All life forms seem to pursue survival and LIFE. Our species likewise pursues LIFE and is still in a Darwinian survival quest. Our major Civilizations, which represent the current organization of the collective mind of our species, are oriented towards LIFE. The West, which engages the left brain more than the others, has been painfully shown (Dark Ages) that it must include a strong orientation towards LIFE, which comes from our right brain.

LIFE and Homo sapiens

Our species, even with our wondrous left brain, remains oriented towards the LIFE that comes to us from our right brain. Darwinian survival of any species depends upon survival of the group. The sense of "group" is deeply embedded in vision-based cognition. It is not a coincidence that our greatest satisfaction comes when we satisfy or meet group needs.

Survival of the species depends upon meeting the group needs…this is a part of all animals, we humans, and, indeed, all forms of Life.

One thing Homo sapiens apparently must do is maintain a central orientation towards LIFE. LIFE must be central and must be honored. Given the perspective about Life and the universe as we understand it,

Homo sapiens appear to have no choice in this matter. Simply stated, we *are* oriented towards LIFE and cannot change that.

It is tempting to think that Homo sapiens would be best served if the intra-group and inter-group relationships (between and within Civilizations) were smooth. However, it seems more likely that agitation within and between groups is good for further development, just as healthy competition is required for business. Pursuit of LIFE seems to necessarily promote some competition and conflict.

LIFE fosters Darwinian competition between and within species. The fittest individuals survive, and also the fittest species survive. Pursuit of LIFE is the drive behind Darwinian survival. Pursuit of LIFE seems to necessarily promote competition, and competition results in conflict. This conflict is demonstrated by extinction of Cambrian-era Trilobytes, rams butting their heads, capitalistic business competition, and civilization conflicts. Pursuit of LIFE creates conflict. Belief in God is also oriented towards LIFE. Many intra-species conflicts, called "wars" have been fought in the name of God. God is LIFE.

LIFE comes to us from our right brain. Our right brain sense of group is the *Homo sapiens* group mind, and the role it plays is somewhat different in each of its groups (called "Civilizations"). The instinctual concept of "group" also necessarily creates the concept of "non-group", and hence is a strong basis for "us" and "them" and a basis for competition. The pursuit of LIFE necessarily creates conflict between Civilizations. The pursuit of LIFE necessarily creates conflict between groups within Civilizations. The pursuit of LIFE is necessary for survival. The pursuit of LIFE makes us more survivable. The pursuit of LIFE makes us better.

> *Striving towards LIFE is the collective objective of life on this planet. The pursuit of LIFE, coming from our right brain, causes competition and makes us better because of it.*

Homo sapiens seem destined to continue with conflict between its Civilizations. If species survival were challenged by extra-terrestrial beings, then friction between species groups (Civilizations) would become secondary and the Civilizations would work more cooperatively. If *Homo sapiens* survival is threatened by a Malthusian future of over-population and dwindling resources, then it would probably lead to a Darwinian struggle for survival between Civilizations.

Because of its left brain strength, as evidenced by science and technology, Western Civilization seems best suited to prepare for Darwinian conflict with an extra-terrestrial opponent; it also seems best suited for expansion of *Homo sapiens* to other parts of the universe. Because of their greater incorporation of the right brain and sense of group, Islamic and Eastern civilizations seem better suited to survive in the Malthusian scenario. The different strengths and weaknesses of *Homo sapiens* groups appear to improve the survivability odds of our species. We are better prepared for unknown future events because pursuit of LIFE and the ensuing intra-species competition between Civilizations has prepared *Homo sapiens* for a wider array of eventualities. Pursuit of LIFE is Darwinian and necessarily improves survival chances.

LIFE and the Individual

All species exist in the form of a relatively large number of individuals. Each species pursues LIFE – not by choice, but by the charter that is within it. Each species is comprised of groups, which in turn are comprised of individuals. Individuals within a species, such as you and I, seem the lowest quantum unit of a species.

The individuals within a species each contain different genetic make-ups, as the genes are scrambled in the reproductive process. Darwinian competition between individuals and between the groups to which they belong, sorts out the most successful genetic combinations to strengthen the success and survivability of the group and the species.

Do we, as individuals, have any volitional control or affect upon the direction of our Life as we pursue LIFE? Is the future destined?. i.e. is our fate already cast and unalterable, or can we choose to alter Life's directions? Can we will a difference in life's pursuits? Do we have Free Will?

It *feels* as if I have a choice in my Life. I also believe that I have been able to alter the direction of my Life because of choices I have made.

Pursuit of LIFE has resulted in development of speech and the cognitive skills based thereupon, i.e. pursuit of LIFE has resulted in the evolution of Homo sapiens. Our left brain has evolved as Life pursues LIFE. In fact, the left brain has demonstrated its Darwinian prowess in only 30,000 years. Our left brain is the most recent, and most effective, Darwinian competitor yet seen on this planet. Our left brain is not "unnatural', it has been developed by Life as it has pursued LIFE.

It seems plausible, and Darwinian, to enable individual humans to alter the path taken by Civilizations and hence the species. Each individual acts according to its genetic make-up and the base abilities, experiences, and choices they make. Our species has already demonstrated that individuals can make a difference. From Socrates, Buddha, and Confucius to Gandhi, Hitler, and Steve Jobs, individuals have altered the direction of human life on this planet. I choose to *believe* they each made left brain decisions that affected their influential actions.

The alternative to Free Will is that all is pre-determined and there is a Destiny, regardless of choice. It is possible that every future human decision could be known if we knew the entire data base regarding genetic make-up, all past interactions and the effects each interaction had on the behavior patterns. We would also need to have the genetic and behavioral data for all others in the world, and understand the individual and group interactions. The argument against free will says that, if we had all of those data, then we could know future behaviors; i.e. the future is pre-destined. With the growth in data management over the past 50 years, it no longer seems impossible to acquire this magnitude of data. Maybe, someday, we will be able to know whether behavior is pre-destined. I doubt it and I suspect there will always be more unanswered questions once we arrive there.

I choose to accept that we each have free will. It *feels* as if we have free will, and each of us *believe* we have been able to make Life altering decisions with our left brain. Also, we cannot know that we <u>don't</u> have free will, so it seems advantageous to choose to act as if we have it.

We should act as if we have free will. This seems to work and it feels correct.

Since *Homo sapiens* pursue LIFE, and individuals contribute to that pursuit of the species, the summed contribution of individuals contributes to the pursuit of LIFE. Just as our species pursues LIFE, it seems advisable that individual behavior is also in pursuit of LIFE.

We should each pursue LIFE that comes to us from the right brain portion of our mind. This gives us the greatest satisfaction and results in the best individual contributions to our groups and species.

Pursuing LIFE

Life comes to our mind from the vision-based right brain. It is non-verbal, so we can only feel it and can't hear or think it. But, it (Life) is there; we *do* feel it. It feels like an ultimate truth and understanding. For many people on this planet it is God; for others it is acknowledgement of Tao or Enlightenment. For me, it is Yes to LIFE.

Jill Bolte Taylor gives a vivid first-hand description of the differences between our right and left brains. She is a behavioral scientist who had a stroke of her left brain, recovered, and was able to give a lucid and passionate description of her left and right brain consciousness as her left brain was being cut-off by the stroke. By her descriptions, there is harmony and beauty in the right brain. The video is entitled Stroke of Insight and can be found on the web.

The right brain cognitive state is happy, beautiful, and harmonious. This is similar to meditative states. We become in greater touch with Life when we become attuned to our right brain.

Oprah Winfrey has made outstanding statements that describe the power and significance of pursuing LIFE.

"Your calling isn't something that somebody can tell you about. It's what you feel. It's a part of your life force. It is the thing that gives you juice. The

thing that you are supposed to do. And nobody can tell you what that is. You know it inside yourself."

Oprah Winfrey, Commencement Speech at Howard University, 2007.

"And how do you know when you're doing something right? How do you know that? It feels so. What I know now is that feelings are really your GPS system for life. When you're supposed to do something or not supposed to do something, your emotional guidance system lets you know. The trick is to learn to check your ego at the door and start checking your gut instead."

Oprah Winfrey, Commencement Speech at Stanford University, 2008.

The truths and meaning of Life, and the pursuit of LIFE, come to us from our right brain. We must say "Yes" to it. We must also say "Yes" to our magnificent left brain for the wonder that it is.

POSTSCRIPT

This has been an awe-inspiring journey for me. Trying to contemplate the universe, human nature, god, the past, present, and future - these topics can quickly make one feel small and insignificant.

I have gained insights into my own consciousness, and the facts that it has vision-based and speech-based components that are very separate and observable through introspection. Our human left brain has been developed by Life as it pursues LIFE and is amazing; for the first time a life form on this planet is able to contemplate the issues addressed in this book. Our right brain cognition has developed straight from the non-verbal animal world. Human behavior and human history can be interpreted and viewed by understanding our individual and collective vision-based and speech-based cognition. These were aha discoveries for me.

I have gained the insight that, although *Homo sapiens* are very special because we have quickly ascended to Life prominence on this planet, in the end we are still simply another species of Life. In this latter respect, *Homo sapiens* pursue something called LIFE and engage in the ensuing Darwinian struggle along with all other species. Our major civilizations are simply groups within our species. Each group (Civilization) incorporates *pursuit of LIFE* into its basic structure of the group mind. Our species remains oriented towards LIFE, as it should….and must.

I am humbled by the enormity of Life and LIFE, and the relative insignificance of my Life. I have a much better understanding of my role in Life. Although my role in Life seems small, it is my responsibility to do my best for furtherance of Life as we pursue LIFE. I want to have strong shoulders to support others, and can choose to allow myself to do so.

The feeling of one-ness with LIFE occurs most readily, and not surprisingly, when communing with nature or experiencing true and romantic love. LIFE is beautiful and harmonious. I say Yes to LIFE.

Sources

The Holy Bible, King James Version.
Birth of the Earth, How the Earth was Made, from the Complete Season Two, History Channel
Boeree, George C. . Chapter on Carl Jung in "Personality Theories". E-textbook, 1997.
Bloom, Stephen G. Postville – a Clash of Cultures in Heartland America. Harcourt, Inc, New York, 2000.
Bownds, Deric M. Biology of the Mind – Origins and Structures of Mind, Brain, and Consciousness. Fitzgerald Science Press, Bethesda, 1999.
Carnegie, Dale. How to Stop Worrying and Start Living. Pocket Books, NY, NY, 1990.
Cobo, Bernabé, Historia del Nuevo Mundo, bk 12., as cited by Wikipedia, Jan 2011. Also appears on several other web-sites.
Cooper, JM. Plato Complete Works. Hackett Publishing, Indianapolis, 1997.
de Boer, Bart. Evolution of Speech and Its Acquisition. Adaptive Behavior 2005 13: 281, 2005.
Diamond, Jared. Guns, Germs, and Steel – the Fates of Human Societies. W. W. Norton and Company, New York, 1999.
Edelman, Gerald M. Wider Than the Sky. Yale University Press, New Haven, 2004.
Edman, Irwin. The Works of Plato, the Jowett Translation. The Modern Library, New York, 1928.
Egypt's 10 Greatest Discoveries, DVD, Discovery Channel.
Frankl, Viktor E. Man's Search for Meaning. Washington Square Press, New York, 1959.

Horney, Karen. Neurosis and Human Growth – The Struggle Toward Self-Realization. W. W. Norton and Company, New York, 1950.

Huntington, Samuel P. The Clash of Civilization and the Remaking of the World Order. Simon and Schuster, New York, 1996.

Jaynes, Julian. The Origin of Consciousness in the Breakdown of the Bicameral Mind. Houghton Mifflin Company, Boston, 1976, 1990.

Jung, Carl Gustav. Psychological Types. Princeton University Press, Princeton, NJ, 1971.

Kushner, Harold. When All You've Ever Wanted Isn't Enough – the Search for a Life that Matters. Pocket Books, New York, 1986.

Luders, Eileen; Thompson, Paul M; Toga Arthur W. The Development of the Corpus Callosum in the Healthy Human Brain. The Journal of Neuroscience, 18 August 2010, 30(33): 10985-10990.

Mithen, Steve. The Prehistory of the Mind – the Cognitive Origins of Art and Science. Thames and Hudson Ltd, London, 1996.

Nilsson, Dan-Eric. (2011). In Encyclopædia Britannica. Retrieved from http://www.britannica.com/EBchecked/topic/1475520/Dan-Eric-Nilsson

Nisbett, Richard E. The Geography of Thought. The Free Press, New York, 2003.

Pagels, Elaine. The Gnostic Gospels. Vintage Books, New York, 1989.

Plachetzki, David C; Degnan, Bernard M; Oakley, Todd H. The Origins of Novel Protein Interactions during Animal Opsin Evolution. PLoS ONE 2(10): e1054. doi:10.1371/journal.pone.0001054, 2007.

Ramachandran V. S. and Blakeslee S. Phantoms in the Brain: Probing the Mysteries of the Human Mind. Harper Perennial, New York, 1999.

Roberts, J.M. A Short History of the World. Oxford University Press, New York, 1993.

Scarpari, Maurizio. Ancient China: Chinese Civilizations from the Origins to the Tang Dynasty. VMB Publishers, White Star, Italy, 2006

Townsley, Graham, DVD editor. Becoming Human, Unearthing our Earliest Ancestors. Public Broadcasting System, 2009.

Van Doren, Charles. A History of Knowledge. Ballantine Books, New York, 1992.

Wells, Spencer. The Journey of Man, a Genetic Odyssey. Random House, New York, 2003.

Wells. Spencer, editor DVD. Journey of Man. Public Broadcasting System, 2003.

Wilson, Edward O. Consilience – the Unity of Knowledge. Vintage Books, New York, 1998.

Young-Eisendrath, Polly and Dawson, Terence. The Cambridge Companion to Jung. Cambridge University Press, Cambridge, UK, 1997.

Acknowledgements

It is not possible for me to list or properly acknowledge all of those who have provided strong shoulders for this book. Lonny Harrison and Terry Schultz have been life-long friends who have helped me to think my way through life's issues. My sister, Patricia Reppenhagen, and Melissa Hill have helped me to respect and understand the right brain. David Kellner, Palmer Cook, Shawn Curtner, and Sally Haltom have all reviewed some of these writings and provided invaluable comments, thoughts and suggestions.

I also owe early inspiration from Joyce Bleby who introduced me to eastern thought and a set of mantras that altered my ways of thinking. She also introduced me to the writings of Karen Horney that have been helpful. In the same vein, the experiences and writings of Viktor Frankl were powerful in understanding the essence of our humanity, although the more recent works of Harold Kushner had an even greater impact on these insights. I thank Michael Harris for introducing me to him...and also for being a strong voice of reason and compassion in my life.

Some of my earliest inspirations came from reading Julian Jaynes, who really caused me to think about the human mind and its development. Edward Wilson was excellent follow-up reading. Steve Mithen provided very useful thoughts about early development of the mind. Jared Diamond added a firm background for understanding the environments from which we have evolved and many other developmental issues.

Two writers have particularly helped to crystallize my thoughts on our human development: Samuel Huntington has written an excellent book on civilizations in our current world and Charles Van Doren has reviewed the development of Western Civilization with tremendous insight. J.M. Roberts has also provided a very good narrative of human history. Elaine

Pagels, in *The Gnostic Gospels*, has provided excellent documentation and thoughts about a special period in our history.

I also thank several friends and colleagues who took a course that I taught, entitled "Vision, Mind and Civilization". Comments and critique by Hannu Laukkanen, John Hayes, Johannes Tan, Marti Fredericks, Cathy Evans, Collin Robillard, and Patrick Campaign were particularly useful in helping me to refine and focus my ideas. Trudy Amery helped to show me the depths of our right brain and the beauty in it. Ruth Anne McCullough was helpful by editing this manuscript. Susan Pachuta has shown me how to more fully experience the right brain and has provided valuable insights for me to consider as I have finalized these writings.

And, finally, in addition to the contemporaries listed above, I stand on the very strong shoulders of the many people that have gone before us and built our civilizations. I have mentioned some of them in this book, but the number mentioned is woefully incomplete.

18885134R00116

Made in the USA
Charleston, SC
25 April 2013